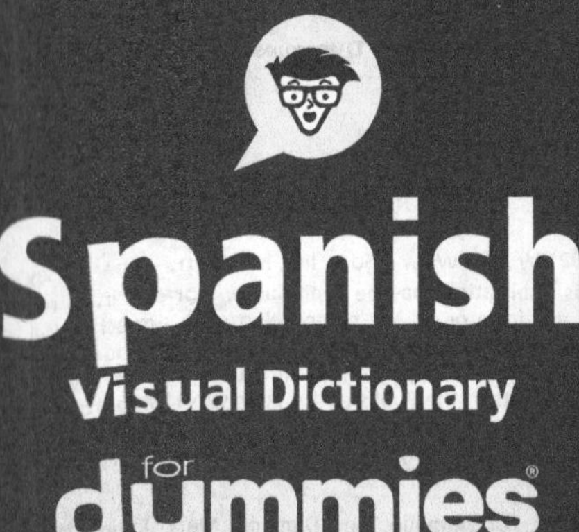

Spanish Visual Dictionary for dummies®

WILEY

Spanish Visual Dictionary For Dummies®

Published by
John Wiley & Sons, Inc.
111 River St.
Hoboken, NJ 07030-5774
www.wiley.com

For general information on our other products and services, or how to create a custom *For Dummies* book for your business or organization, please contact our Business Development Department in the U.S. at 877-409-4177, contact info@dummies.biz, or visit www.wiley.com/go/custompub. For information about licensing the *For Dummies* brand for products or services, contact BrandedRights&Licenses@Wiley.com.

Library of Congress Control Number: 2021933184

ISBN : 978-1-119-71712-6

SKY10025773_060821

Introduction

This *Visual Dictionary For Dummies* is your ideal travel companion. It can be carried conveniently and consulted quickly; all you have to do is show the picture of the thing you're talking about or of the situation you wish to describe, and presto! And since the pictures are accompanied by the corresponding English words and their Spanish translations, you will also be able to learn a lot of new vocabulary!

Sounds, Rhythm, and Intonation

Spanish and English have a lot in common, including a common history. While Spanish is a Romance language and English is Germanic, a portion of the English language was influenced by Romance sources and vice-versa. Many centuries ago, as these languages were still fairly new, they began to merge as the Germanic and Roman people increased communication. This common history means our two vocabularies also have much in common — in fact, 30 percent to 40 percent of all words in English have a related word in Spanish.

The sounds: the vowels

Simple vowels

In English, the vowels are divided into two groups: the so-called long or tense vowels, and the so-called short or lax vowels. Spanish does away with the distinction — all vowels are pronounced alike.

- **agua (A):** The Spanish "a" sound in **agua** is the same as the "a" sound in English word **father**.
- **deber (E):** The Spanish "e" is pronounced like the "eh" in the English word **web**.
- **dificil (I):** The Spanish "i" is pronounced like the "ee" in the English word **deed**.
- **otoño (O):** The Spanish "o" sound in **otoño** is a good match for the long "o" sound in the English word **oak**.
- **sur (U):** The Spanish "u" sound in **sur** matches the vowel sound we have in the English word **tool**.

Blending your words

Yes, Spanish speakers tend to talk fast! That means words tend to blend together — and you sometimes don't make a clear distinction from the end of one word and the beginning of another. This is especially true in the following cases:

- When the last letter of a word is the same as the first letter of the next word
- When the last letter of a word is a consonant and the first letter of the next word is a vowel
- When the last letter of a word is a vowel and the first letter of the next word is a vowel

Intonation

Intonation in Spanish — deciding which syllable to stress — is particularly difficult for English speakers. Words are stressed in a different rhythm than in English. Don't worry, though; if you follow a few simple guidelines, you'll soon be speaking Spanish like a native:

- Words that end with vowels are stressed on the next-to-last syllable.
- Words that end with an "n" or an "s" are also stressed on the next-to-last syllable.
- Words that end with a consonant that is not an "n" or an "s" are stressed on the last syllable.
- Exceptions to the rules above are marked with an accent over the vowel to be stressed.

The sounds: the consonants

Most Spanish consonants match the sound of English exactly, but you'll need to pay particular attention to some consonants that are tricky for English speakers to pronounce.

- **"ll":** The "ll" has the same sound that the letter "j" does in a lot of English words — **juice**, **jade**, **June**, and **July**, for example. That means **juice** and **lluvia** (*rain*) both start with the same sound.

- **"y":** When you have a "y" at the beginning or middle of a word, the "y" sound is the same as the Spanish "ll" or the English "j" in **juice**. When you have a "y" at the end of the word, it acts as a vowel sound just like the "ee" in **eerie**.
- **"b" and "v":** This may take some getting used to. In Spanish, there is absolutely no difference between the sound of "b" and the sound of "v" — it will always be a "b" sound. That means **Venezuela** actually sounds like **Benezuela**.
- **"h":** Spanish speakers don't generally pronounce the letter "h." The one exception is when it is used in combination with a "c," as in "ch." When that occurs, it has the "ch" sound we have in English for **chair** or **choose**. (Think **chimichanga** or **churros**.)
- **"j":** The "j" sound is the same as the basic "h" sound in English; think **Javier**. There is a subtle difference depending on where you are — parts of Latin America versus regions in Spain, to be more specific. In some areas — El Salvador, for example — the "j" sounds very much like the English "h"; in Guatemala, the "j" sound still sounds like an "h," but it has a more ragged, raspy feel to it.

- **"r":** When used at the beginning, middle, or end of a word, Spanish speakers "roll their rs," which is something English speakers rarely do. The closest we come is when we try to imitate a dog by saying **rrruuuufff rrrruuuufff!** That means the "r" in the Spanish word **roja** is more like the "r" in **rrrrrrrro rrrrrrrro rrrrrrrrosey, goodbye.**
- **'ñ':** The "n with a little mustache on" will be a new phenomenon for English speakers. Just think of it as an "ny" combination, as in the English word **lanyard**. (The accent mark on the "n" is known as a *tilde.*)
- **"z":** Here, regional differences again play a role. If you are speaking Spanish in Latin America, there's really no difference between "z" and "s" sounds, but if you're in Spain and you want to pronounce the "z" sound correctly, you need talk as if you have a lisp, changing the "z" for a "th," as in the English word **thick**. Some words that'll help you practice the "z" sound are **cereza** *(cherry),* **zapatos** *(shoes),* and **Suiza** *(Switzerland).*

¡Vamos!

Let's go!

El avión
Plane

El aeropuerto
Airport

El avión
Airplane

La compañía aérea
Airline

El mostrador
Ticket counter

El equipaje
Luggage

El equipaje de mano
Carry-on luggage

El bolso de viaje
Travel bag

La maleta
Suitcase

El carrito
[Luggage] cart

Productos líquidos
Liquid products

El control de seguridad
Security checkpoint

El ciudadano de los EE UU
U.S. citizen

El avión
Plane

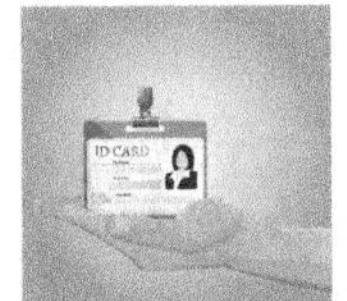

El carné de identidad
Identity card

El pasaporte
Passport

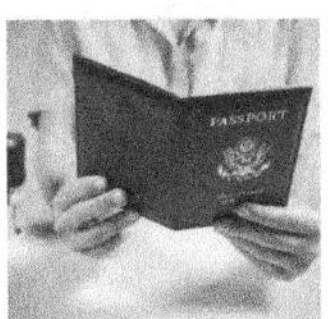

El control de pasaportes
Passport control

La facturación
Check-in

La aduana
Customs

El billete de ida y vuelta
Round-trip ticket

La puerta de embarque
Gate

La tarjeta de embarque
Boarding card

El embarque
Boarding

La salida de emergencia
Emergency exit

El piloto
Pilot

La azafata
Flight attendant

El avión
Plane

El vuelo
Flight

De ventanilla
(Seat) by the window

De pasillo
(Seat) on the aisle

El asiento
Seat

El cinturón de seguridad
Seat belt

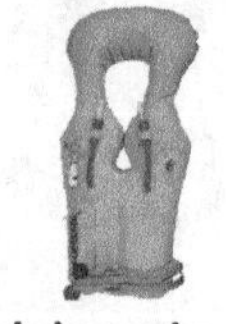

El chaleco salvavidas
Life vest

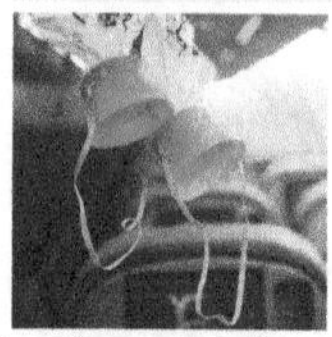

La máscara de oxígeno
Oxygen mask

El despegue
Take-off

El aterrizaje
Landing

La llegada
Arrivals

Carrusel de equipaje
Baggage carousel

El autobús
Shuttle bus

El avión

Plane

Frases clave	Key phrases
¿A qué hora sale/llega?	What time do we leave?/ arrive?
¿Dónde está el mostrador de Iberia?	Where is the Iberia ticket office/desk?
¿Dónde se factura el equipaje?	Where do we check our luggage?
¿Puedo llevar esta bolsa como equipaje de mano?	Can I take this bag as carry-on luggage?
¿A qué hora y dónde es el embarque?	At what time and at what gate is boarding?/When do we board and at which gate?
¿Podría darme los horarios de los vuelos para . . . ?	Could you give me the flight schedules for . . . ?
¿Cuánto dura el vuelo?	How long does the flight last?
¿Dónde se recoge el equipaje?	Where is luggage pick-up/ baggage claim?
He olvidado algo en el avión.	I left something on the plane.
Me falta una maleta.	I am missing a suitcase.
Mi equipaje no ha llegado.	My luggage hasn't arrived.

El tren y los transportes públicos

The train and public transport

La estación
Station

El andén
Platform

La vía
Track

El tren
Train

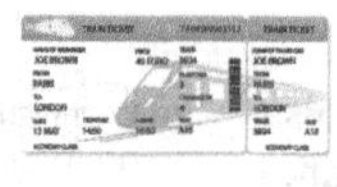

El billete de tren
Train ticket

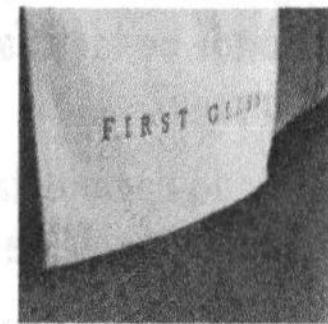

La primera clase
First class

La segunda clase
Second class

El asiento
Seat

La litera
Bunk/berth

El vagón restaurante
Dining car

La información
Information

La reserva
Booking

El tren y los transportes públicos

The train and public transport

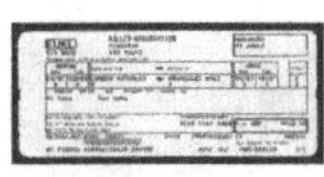

El billete de ida/ de ida y vuelta
One-way/round-trip ticket

La salida
Departure

El retraso
Delay

La cancelación
Cancellation

El horario
Schedule/timetable

Picar
To punch (a ticket)

Subir al tren
To get on the train

Bajar del tren
To get off the train

La llegada
Arrival

El revisor
Conductor

La cola de espera
Waiting line

La ventanilla de venta de billetes
Ticket window/booth

El tren y los transportes públicos

The train and public transport

La máquina de boletos
Ticket machine

El transbordo
Connection

El autobús
Bus

El conductor de bus
Bus driver

La parada de autobús
Bus stop

El metro
Metro/subway

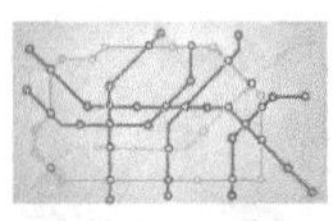

La línea de metro
Metro/subway line

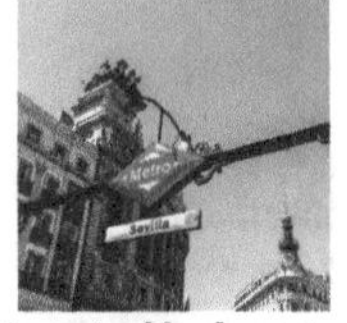

La estación de metro
Metro/subway station

El cercanías
Commuter train

El tranvía
Trolley/streetcar

El funicular
Cable car

El tren y los transportes públicos

The train and public transport

Transportation

Frases clave	Key phrases
¿De qué vía sale el tren para . . . ?	On what track does the train for . . . leave?
Quiero un asiento en el sentido de la marcha.	I would like a seat facing the direction of travel.
¿El tren está retrasado?	Is the train running late?
¿Me puede dar un plano de los autobuses / del metro?	Can you give me a bus/ subway route map?
¿Qué autobús / metro hay que coger para ir a . . . ?	Which bus/subway do I need to take to get to . . . ?
¿Es directo o hay que hacer algún cambio?	Is it direct, or do I have to change buses/trains?
¿A qué hora es el primer / último metro?	What time is the first/last subway?
Perdone, ¿está libre este asiento?	Excuse me, is this seat free?
¿Dónde me tengo que bajar?	Where do I have to get off?
¿Hay autobuses nocturnos?	Are there any overnight buses?
¿El 18 me deja en la estación central?	Will the 18 take me to the central station?

El coche
Car

El coche
Car

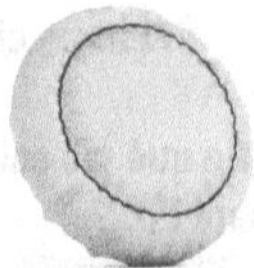

El carné de conducir
Driver's license

El Airbag
Airbag®

El cinturón de seguridad
Seat belt

La rueda
Wheel

El freno
Brake

El retrovisor
Rearview mirror

El volante
Steering wheel

El salpicadero
Dashboard

El motor
Engine

El maletero
Trunk

La luz
Headlight

El coche
Car

El depósito
Fuel/gas tank

La matrícula
License plate

El limpiaparabrisas
Windshield wipers

La carretera
Road

El semáforo
Traffic light

El mapa de carreteras
Road map

La autopista
Highway

La autovía
Expressway

La salida de la autopista
Off-ramp

El acceso a la autopista
On-ramp

La intersección de autopistas
Highway interchange/junction

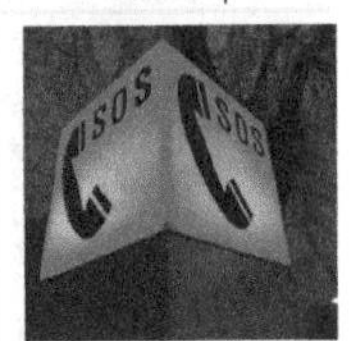

El teléfono de emergencia
Emergency phone

El coche
Car

El área de descanso
Rest stop/area

El peaje
Toll (booth)

El atasco
Traffic jam

Prohibido aparcar
No parking

El desvío
Detour

Las obras
Roadwork/work zone

El túnel
Tunnel

El accidente de coche
Car accident

El pinchazo
Flat tire

La avería
Breakdown/car trouble

La grúa
Tow truck/wrecker

El tráfico
Traffic

El coche
Car

El aparcamiento
Parking

Frases clave	Key phrases
¿Dónde hay una gasolinera / una toma de corriente?	Where is a service station/ charging station?
Quiero llenar el depósito	I would like to fill up.
Surtidor número . . .	Pump number . . .
El coche no arranca.	The car won't start.
¿Me puede acercar a un taller?	Can you take me to a garage/repair shop?
Hace un ruido raro.	It [the car] is making a strange noise.
Me he quedado sin gasolina.	I am out of gas/I ran out of gas.

El alquiler de coches

Car rental

La agencia de alquiler
Car rental agency

El seguro
Insurance

Dos / cuatro puertas
Two/four doors

El sedán
Sedan

El coche familiar
Station wagon

El monovolumen
Minivan

El vehículo todoterreno
Sport utility vehicle/SUV

El descapotable
Convertible

El coupé
Coupe/sports car

La transmisión automática
Automatic transmission

La caja de cambios manual
Standard transmission/stick shift

El aire acondicionado
Air conditioner

El alquiler de coches

Car rental

To rent/lease a car
Alquilar un coche

To drive
Conducir

Technical/ mechanical problem
Un problema técnico

Key phrases	Frases clave
Quiero un coche económico con GPS.	I want an economy car with GPS.
¿Cuánto cuesta por día / por semana?	How much is the fee per day/per week?/What is the rate per day/per week?
¿Me puede enseñar el catálogo de modelos y precios?	May I see the catalog of models and prices?
Quiero alquilar un coche / una escúter por dos horas.	I would like to rent a car/a scooter for two hours.
¿Dónde alquilan coches?	Where can you rent cars?
Quiero devolver el coche a . . .	I want to return the car at . . .

El taxi

Taxi

El taxi
Taxi

La parada de taxis
Taxi stand

El taxista
Taxi driver/cabbie

Frases clave	Key phrases
¿Dónde hay una parada de taxis?	Where is a taxi stand?
¿Puede pedirme un taxi?	Can you call/order me a taxi?
Quisiera ir a . . .	I would like to go to . . .
Puede parar aquí / en el semáforo, gracias.	Please stop here/at the traffic light.
¿Cuánto costará la carrera de aquí al centro?	How much is the trip from here to downtown?
Lléveme a esta dirección / al aeropuerto, por favor.	Please take me to this address/to the airport.
Espéreme un momento, por favor.	Please wait a moment for me.
Quédese con el cambio.	Keep the change.

La bicicleta
Bicycle

La bicicleta
Bicycle

El casco
Helmet

El sillín
Seat

El manillar
Handlebars

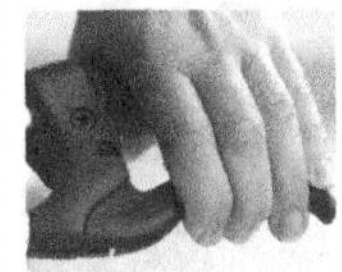

El freno
Brake

El pedal
Pedal

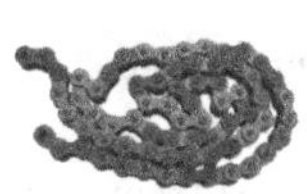

La cadena
Chain

El neumático
Tire

La llanta
Rim

El timbre
Bell

El kit de reparación
Repair kit

La bomba (para bicicleta)
(Bicycle) pump

La bicicleta
Bicycle

El carril bici
Bike path

La cadena
Bicycle lock

La cantimplora
Water bottle

El chaleco de seguridad
Safety vest

El portabicicletas
Bike rack

La bicicleta de montaña
Mountain bike

Frases clave	Key phrases
Querríamos alquilar bicicletas.	We would like to rent some bicycles.
Mi bicicleta ha descarrilado.	My bicycle chain has derailed.
¿Dónde está el carril bici?	Where is the bike path?
Me gustaría montar en bicicleta.	I would like to go bicycling.
¿Tiene un parche para mi neumático?	Do you have a tire patch?

¡Hola!

Basic Communication

Decir hola
Saying hello

¡Hola!
Hello!

¡Buenos días!
Good day! (Good morning!)

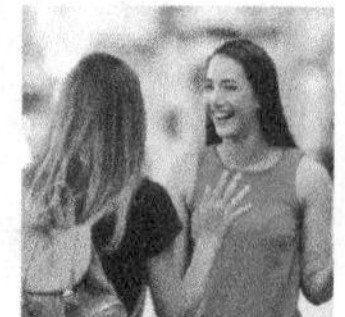

¿Cómo estás / está?
How are you (doing)?

¡Buenas tardes!
Good day! (Good afternoon!)

¡Buenas noches!
Good evening!
(when it's night)

El apretón de manos
Handshake

Besarse
To kiss

Decir hola

Saying hello

Frases clave	Key phrases
¿Qué tal?	How's it going?
¿Cómo estás / está?	How are you (doing)?
Muy bien, gracias.	Very well, thank you.
¿Y tú / usted?	And you?
Da recuerdos a . . .	Say hi to . . . /Give my regards to . . .
Estoy encantado(a) de conocerte.	It's nice to meet you.

Pedir cortésmente, agradecer y disculparse

Asking politely, saying thank you, and apologizing

Por favor
Excuse me/pardon me (to attract someone's attention)

Perdone
Pardon me/sorry (to excuse yourself)

Por favor
Please

Muchas gracias
Thank you very much

¡Bienvenido(a)!
Welcome!

¡Excelente!
Excellent!

Frases clave	Key phrases
Perdone que le moleste.	I apologize for bothering/ disturbing you.
Lo siento mucho.	I'm very sorry.
No pasa nada.	It's nothing/no problem.
Gracias por su ayuda.	Thank you for your help.
Le estoy muy agradecido(a) por . . .	I am very grateful to you for . . .
De nada.	Don't mention it.
No hay de qué.	You're welcome.
Estaba muy bueno.	It was very good.

Decir adiós

Saying farewell

¡Adiós!
Goodbye!

¡Buenas noches!
Good night!

¡Hasta mañana!
Until tomorrow!

¡Hasta la próxima!
(See you) later!

¡Hasta pronto!
See you soon!

¡Buen viaje!
Have a good trip!

Frases clave	Key phrases
Tengo que irme.	I have to go.
¡Hasta ahora!	Very soon!
¡Hasta luego!	Later!
¡Hasta el año que viene!	Until next year!

Los problemas de comunicación

Communication problems

Más despacio
Please slow down

¿Habla inglés?
Do you speak English

Español(a)
Spanish

Frases clave	Key phrases
¿Me lo puede repetir?	Can you repeat that?
No hablo español.	I do not speak Spanish.
No entiendo.	I do not understand.
Hablo un poquito español.	I speak a little (bit of) Spanish.
¿Puedes deletrearlo / escribírmelo?	Can you spell it/write it for me?
¿Cómo se llama esto?	What is that?
¿Qué significa . . . ?	What does . . . mean?

El horario

Time

A tiempo
On time

Temprano(a)
Early

Retrasado(a)
Late

La hora
Hour

El minuto
Minute

El cuarto de hora
Quarter hour

La media hora
Half hour

La mañana
Morning

El mediodía
Noon

La tarde
Afternoon

La tarde, la noche
Evening (before/ after sunset)

El día
Day

El horario

Time

La noche
Night

La puesta de sol
Sunset

Frases clave	Key phrases
Tengo hora a las diez.	I have an appointment at 10 o'clock.
Me gustaría pedir hora.	I would like to make an appointment.
¡Qué tarde es!	It's getting late!
¿Qué hora es?	What time is it?
Son las cinco menos cuarto.	It is quarter to five.
Son las cuatro y media.	It is four-thirty/half past four.
Son las doce del mediodía / de la noche.	It is 12 noon/midnight.

¡Mi camino!

Getting around

Algunos puntos de referencia

Landmarks, reference points

La oficina de turismo
Tourist office

El mapa
Map

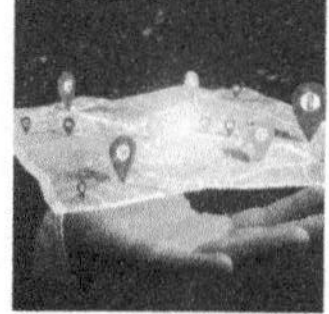

El plano (de la ciudad)
(City) map

El centro (ciudad)
Downtown area

La calle peatonal
Pedestrian street

El barrio
Neighborhood/district

La calle
Street

El cruce
Intersection/crossroad

La rotonda
Roundabout

El paso de cebra
Crosswalk

La acera
Sidewalk

La plaza
Plaza, town square

Algunos puntos de referencia

Landmarks, reference points

El edificio
Building

El río
River

El puerto
Port, harbor

El puente
Bridge

El mercado
Market

El ayuntamiento
City hall

La estación
Station

El estadio
Stadium

El aeropuerto
Airport

El hospital
Hospital

La farmacia
Pharmacy/drug store

El banco
Bank

Algunos puntos de referencia

Landmarks, reference points

La oficina de correos
Post office

El supermercado
Supermarket

Frases clave	Key phrases
¿Tiene un plano de la ciudad?	Do you have a city map?
¿Podría darme documentación en inglés sobre . . . ?	Could I get information in English on . . . ?
¿Cuáles son los principales monumentos?	What are the main monuments?
¿Qué hay para ver por aquí cerca?	What is there to see nearby?
¿Me lo puede indicar en el mapa?	Can you show it to me on the map?
Estoy perdido(a). ¿Puede ayudarme?	I am lost. Can you help me?
¿Me puede indicar en el mapa dónde estamos?	Can you show me where we are on the map?
¿Cuánto se tarda para ir al centro ?	How long does it take to go downtown?
¿Se puede ir andando?	Can you get there by walking?

Las direcciones

Directions

Girar
To turn

Seguir
To follow

Todo recto
Straight

Subir
To climb (stairs)

Bajar
To go down (stairs)

A la derecha
Right

A la izquierda
Left

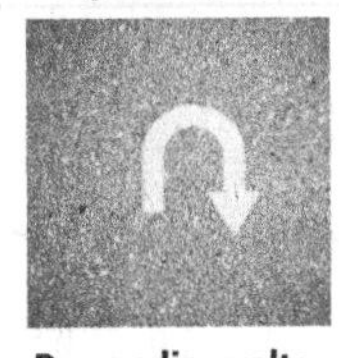

Dar media vuelta
To turn around

Detrás
Behind

Delante
In front

Lejos
Far

Cerca
Near

Las direcciones

Directions

Andando
On foot

Aquí
Here

Allí
(Over) there

Frases clave	Key phrases
¿Es la dirección correcta?	Is this the right way?
¿Al salir de aquí, giramos a la derecha o a la izquierda?	When you leave here, do you turn right or left?
¿Está al norte o al sur?	Is it north or south?
¿Está al este o al oeste?	Is it east or west?
¿Dónde estamos?	Where are we?

Los puntos de interés en la ciudad

Points of interest in the city

El casco antiguo
Historic district

El parque
Park

La fuente
Fountain

La estatua
Statue

El quiosco
Pavilion

El rastro
Flea market

La biblioteca
Library

El teatro
Theater

A ópera
Opera

La catedral
Cathedral

La iglesia
Church

El monasterio
Cloister, monastery

Los puntos de interés en la ciudad

Points of interest in the city

La mezquita
Mosque

La sinagoga
Synagogue

La abadía
Abbey

El castillo
Castle

La fortaleza
Fortress

El palacio
Palace

Las ruinas
Ruins

Las murallas
Ramparts, city walls

El rascacielos
Skyscraper

El zoo
Zoo

El restaurante
Restaurant

El café
Café

Los puntos de interés en la ciudad

Points of interest in the city

El hotel
Hotel

La tienda
Store

Frases clave	Key phrases
¿Hay que pagar?	Do you have to pay?/Is there a fee?
¿Esto es gratis?	Is it free (of charge)?
¿Dónde se compran los billetes?	Where do you buy tickets?
Deme una entrada reducida y una normal, por favor.	Please give me a reduced-price ticket and a full-price admission ticket.
¿Hay visitas guiadas / una audioguía en inglés?	Are there guided tours in English?/Is there an audio guide in English?
¿A qué hora es la siguiente visita guiada?	What time is the next guided tour?
¿Cuánto tiempo dura la visita?	How long does the tour last?

Los aseos públicos

Public toilets

Los servicios
(Public) toilets

El baño
Bathroom (in a house)

El servicio de señoras
Ladies room

El servicio de hombres
Men's room

El servicio de discapacitados
Toilets for people with disabilities/ handicapped bathroom facilities

El cambiador
Changing table

El jabón
Soap

El papel higiénico
Toilet paper

El secador
Hand dryer

Los aseos públicos

Public toilets

Frases clave	Key phrases
¿Dónde está el baño por favor?	Could you please tell me where the bathroom is?
¿Podemos parar aquí para ir a los servicios?	Can we stop here to go to the bathroom?
¿Hay un cambiador en algún lugar?	Is there a changing table around here?

El clima
Weather

El clima
Weather

El cielo
Sky

La temperatura
Temperature

La humedad
Humidity

El calor
Heat

El frío
Cold

El sol
Sun

Soleado
Sunny

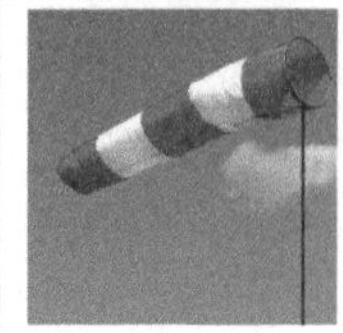

El viento
Wind

La nube
Cloud

La lluvia
Rain

La nieve
Snow

El clima
Weather

La niebla
Fog

La helada
Frost

El relámpago
Lightning

La tormenta
Storm

El clima
Weather

Frases clave	Key phrases
Hace sol / bochorno.	It's sunny/it's scorching.
Hace buen / mal tiempo.	The weather is nice/bad (it's nice out/it's nasty out).
Hace (mucho) calor / frío.	It's (very) hot/cold.
Está nublado.	It's cloudy.
Va a haber tormenta.	A storm is coming.
Llueve / Nieva.	It's raining/it's snowing.
¿Qué tiempo va a hacer mañana?	What's the weather going to be like tomorrow?
¿Cuáles son las previsiones ?	What is the forecast?
Estamos a veinticinco grados.	It's twenty-five degrees.

Los paisajes
Landscapes

El campo
The country(side)

El bosque
Woods, forest

El campo
Field

El árbol
Tree

El prado
Meadow

La montaña
Mountain

La cadena de montañas
The mountains/
mountain range

La colina
Hill

El valle
Valley

El río
River

El arroyo
Stream, creek

El lago
Lake

Los paisajes

Landscapes

La cascada
Waterfall

El océano
Ocean

El mar
Sea

La costa
Seashore, coast

Algunos puntos de referencia

Landmarks, reference points

El parque natural
Nature park

La región
Land/region

El paseo
Walk

El senderismo
Hike, hiking

El mapa
Map

El camino
Trail

La granja
Farm

El puente
Bridge

La cueva
Cave

El pueblo
Village

La iglesia
Church

El molino
(Wind)mill

Algunos puntos de referencia

Landmarks, reference points

La cabaña
Chalet

El refugio
Shelter, mountain cabin

Frases clave	Key phrases
Me gustaría hacer una excursión.	I would like to go on a hike.
¿Hay senderos para hacer excursiones en esta zona?	Are there any hiking trails in the area?
¿El pueblo más cercano queda lejos?	Is it far to the nearest village?
¿De cuántos kilometros es el recorrido?	How many kilometers is the journey?

¡Buen provecho!

Enjoy your meal!

Algunos utensilios de cocina

Kitchenware

 **El vaso** Glass	 **La taza** Cup	 **El plato** Plate
 **El plato sopero** Soup bowl	 **La servilleta de mesa** Napkin	 **El cuchillo** Knife
 **El tenedor** Fork	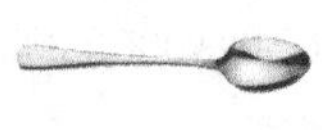 **La cuchara** Spoon	 **Los cubiertos** Cutlery

Algunos utensilios de cocina

Kitchenware

Frases clave	Key phrases
¿Me puede traer una cucharilla?	May I please have a teaspoon?
¿Me puede cambiar el vaso? Está sucio . . .	May I have another glass? This one is dirty . . .
¿Puedo ayudarle a poner / quitar la mesa?	May I help you set/clear the table?

Las diferentes comidas y platos

Different meals and dishes

El desayuno
Breakfast

El almuerzo, la comida
Lunch

La merienda
Snack

La cena
Dinner, supper

El aperitivo
Appetizer

Los entremeses
Hors d'oeuvres

El primer plato
First course

El segundo plato
Main course

El postre
Dessert

Frases clave	Key phrases
¡A comer!	Let's eat!
Tengo hambre.	I'm hungry.
Tengo sed.	I'm thirsty.

El desayuno

Breakfast

El pan
Bread

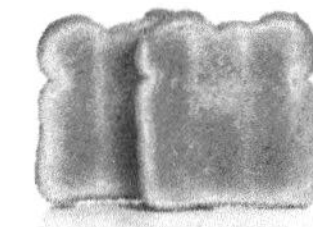

La tostada
Toast

Los cereales
Cereal

El azúcar
Sugar

Los churros con chocolate
Churros with hot chocolate

El cruasán
Croissant

El pan con tomate
Bruschetta

La leche
Milk

El café
Coffee

El café con leche
Café au lait

El té
Tea

El chocolate
Hot cocoa/chocolate

El desayuno

Breakfast

 **La miel** Honey	 **La mantequilla** Butter	 **La mermelada** Jam
 **El zumo de frutas** Fruit juice		

Frases clave	Key phrases
Quiero un café solo / expreso / americano / descafeinado.	I would like black coffee/ espresso/Americano/ decaffeinated coffee.
¿Tiene zumo de naranja ?	Do you have orange juice?

La carne y el embutido

Meats and cold cuts

La costilla
Cutlet, chop

El bistec
Steak

El buey o res
Beef

La ternera
Veal

El cerdo
Pork

El cordero
Lamb

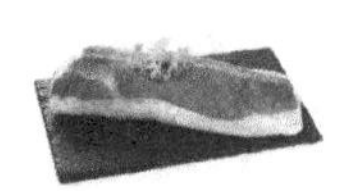

El pato
Duck

El pollo
Chicken

El conejo
Rabbit

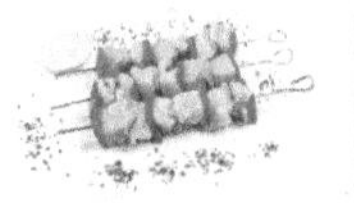

La brocheta
Skewer, shish kabob

La carne picada
Ground meat

La salchicha
Sausage

La carne y el embutido

Meats and cold cuts

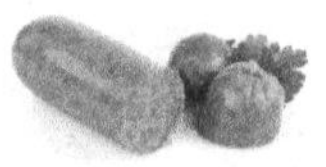

El salchichón
Summer sausage

El jamón
Ham

El jamón de York
Cooked ham

El chorizo
Chorizo

El lomo
Pork loin

El tocino
Bacon

El pescado y los mariscos

Seafood

El pescado
Fish

El bacalao
Cod

El atún
Tuna

La merluza
Hake

La sardina
Sardine

La caballa
Mackerel

El merlán
Whiting

El salmón
Salmon

El lenguado
Sole

La anchoa
Anchovy

El emperador
Swordfish

El lucio
Pike

El pescado y los mariscos

Seafood

La trucha
Trout

La sepia
Cuttlefish

El pulpo
Octopus

El pescado frito
Fried fish

Los palitos de pescado
Fish sticks

Los mariscos
Shellfish

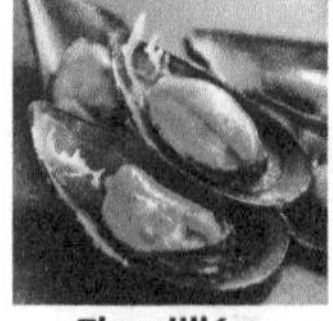

El mejillón
Mussel

La ostra
Oyster

La vieira
Scallop

El cangrejo
Crab

El bogavante
Lobster

La gamba
Shrimp

El pescado y los mariscos

Seafood

La langosta
(Spiny) lobster

El cangrejo de río
Crayfish

Frases clave	Key phrases
¿Qué prefieres, carne o pescado?	Which do you prefer, meat or fish?/Would you rather have meat or fish?
Soy alérgico a los mariscos.	I am allergic to shellfish.
Quiero una carne a la parrilla / a la plancha.	I would like grilled meat.
¿Tiene carne de buey asada?	Do you have roast beef?

Las verduras

Vegetables

Las verduras
Vegetables

La zanahoria
Carrot

La lechuga
Lettuce

La judía verde
Green bean, string bean

El pepino
Cucumber

El pimiento
(Sweet) pepper

El tomate
Tomato

El calabacín
Squash, zucchini

La berenjena
Eggplant

El espárrago
Asparagus

El rábano
Radish

El puerro
Leek

Las verduras
Vegetables

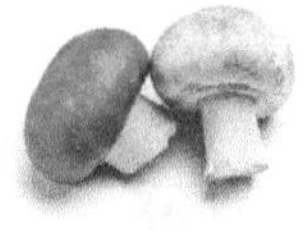

La seta
Mushroom

La col
Cabbage

La coliflor
Cauliflower

El brócoli
Broccoli

La alcachofa
Artichoke

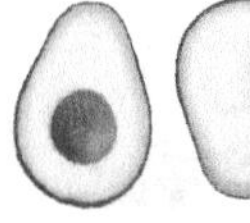

El aguacate
Avocado

La espinaca
Spinach

Los almidones y las legumbres

Starches and legumes

El arroz
Rice

La patata
Potatoe

La pasta
Pasta

La judía blanca
White bean

La sémola de trigo
Semolina

El maíz
Corn

La lenteja
Lentil

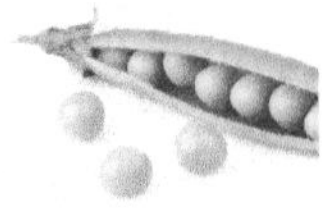

El guisante
Pea

El garbanzo
Chickpea

El haba
Fava bean

Los huevos y los productos lácteos

Eggs and dairy products

El huevo
Egg

La leche
Milk

La mantequilla
Butter

El yogur
Yogurt

La nata
Whipping cream

El queso
Cheese

La fruta

Fruit

La fruta
Fruit

La manzana
Apple

El plátano
Banana

La pera
Pear

La naranja
Orange

La mandarina
Tangerine, mandarin

El pomelo
Grapefruit

El limón/la lima
Lemon/Lime

La uva
Grape

La fresa
Strawberry

La ciruela
Plum

El higola
Fig

La fruta
Fruit

La cereza
Cherry

El melocotón
Peach

El albaricoque
Apricot

El kiwi
Kiwi

La piña
Pineapple

El coco
Coconut

Los frutos de baya
Berries

La grosella
red currant

La mora
Blackberry

La frambuesa
Raspberry

El arándano
Blueberry

El casis
black currant

La fruta y nueces

Fruit and nuts

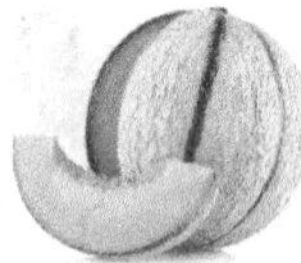

El melón
Melon

La sandía
Watermelon

La uva pasa
Raisin

La almendra
Almond

La avellana
Hazelnut, filbert

El pistacho
Pistachio

El cacahuete
Peanut

La nuez
Walnut

El dátil
Date

La aceituna
Olive

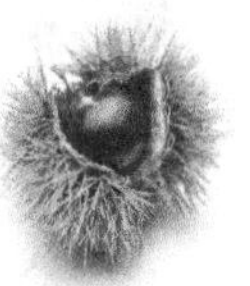

La castaña
Chestnut

Los aliños

Seasonings

La sal
Salt

La pimienta
Pepper

El aceite (de oliva)
(Olive) oil

El vinagre
Vinegar

La mostaza
Mustard

La mayonesa
Mayonnaise

El ketchup
Ketchup

El chile
Hot/chili peppers

La cebolla
Onion

El ajo
Garlic

El chalote
Shallot

El cebollino
Chive

Los aliños
Seasonings

El perejil
Parsley

El tomillo
Thyme

El romero
Rosemary

El laurel
Bay leaf

El perifollo
Chervil

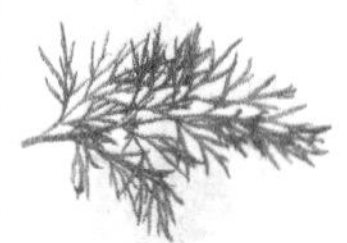

El eneldo
Dill

El cilantro
Coriander, cilantro

El orégano
Oregano

El estragón
Tarragon

La menta
Mint

La albahaca
Basil

La salvia
Sage

Los aliños

Seasonings

El clavo de olor Cloves	**La nuez moscada** Nutmeg	**La canela** Cinnamon

El comino Cumin	**El pimentón** Paprika	**El azafrán** Saffron

Frases clave	Key phrases
Está demasiado picante.	It's too hot (spicy).
No está suficientemente salado.	It needs more salt.
Me gustaría un poco de ketchup por favor.	I'd like some ketchup, please.

Los diferentes restaurantes

The different restaurants

El restaurante
Restaurant

La cervecería
Brewery, alehouse

El albergue
Inn

La tasca
Tapas bar

La marisquería
Seafood restaurant

La bodega
Wine bar

El bar
Bar

El café
Café

Las reservas

Making reservations and ordering

La carta
Menu

La carta de vinos
Wine list

El camarero
Waiter

La mesa
Table

Para llevar
Take-out (to go)

Comer allí
Dine-in (for here)

La zona de fumadores
Smoking area

La zona de no fumadores
No smoking area

Algunos platos

Making reservations and ordering

Frases clave	Key phrases
¿Nos puede recomendar un buen restaurante típico?	Can you recommend a good restaurant that serves local food?
Querría reservar una mesa para dos para esta noche/ para mañana sobre las nueve.	I would like to reserve a table for two for around nine o'clock this evening/ tomorrow evening.
Hemos reservado una mesa a nombre de . . .	We reserved a table under the name of . . .
Tráiganos la carta, por favor.	May we please have a menu?
¿Tienen menús?	Do you have menus?
¿Tienen una mesa libre?	Do you have a free table?

Algunos platos

Some dishes

Los tapas
Tapas, appetizers

La sopa
Soup

La ensalada
Salad

La tortilla de patatas
Potato omelet

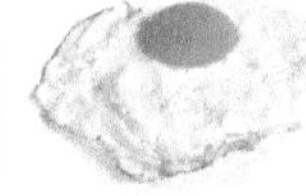

Los huevos fritos
Fried eggs

La pizza
Pizza

La hamburguesa
Hamburger

Las patatas fritas
(French) fries

Las patatas fritas
Potato chips

El plato combinado
Combination plate

Las especialidades locales

Local specialties

Las patatas bravas
Patatas bravas (spiced sautéed potatoes)

El gazpacho
Gazpacho

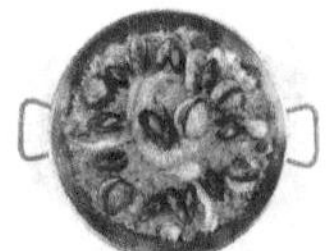

La paella
Paella

El arroz negro
Black rice (with cuttlefish ink)

La fabada
Fabada (pork and bean casserole)

La zarzuela
Fisherman's pot

El cocido madrileño
Madrilenian stew

El pan con tomate
Bruschetta

El rabo de toro
Oxtail

La morcilla
Blood sausage, black pudding

Los riñones al jerez
Sherry kidneys

La fideuá
Paella with pasta

Las especialidades locales

Local specialties

El bocadillo
Mini-sandwich, sub

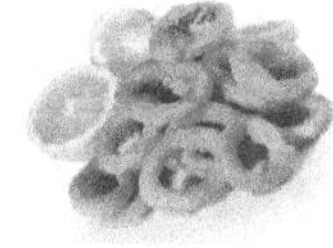

Los calamares a la romana
Roman-style squid, squid fritters

Frases clave	Key phrases
¿Me lo pueden servir con un poco de lechuga en lugar de patatas fritas?	Can I have a small salad instead of fries?/Can I substitute a small salad for fries?
¿Puede ser sin tomate/ sin mayonesa?	Can you hold the tomatoes/the mayonnaise?
Voy a tomar una pizza, pero sin aceitunas/ anchoas.	I will have a pizza, but without olives/anchovies.
Todavía no hemos elegido.	We haven't decided yet.

Los postres
Desserts

El postre
Dessert

La fruta (del tiempo)
(Seasonal) fruit

La macedonia de frutas
Fruit salad

La crema catalana
Crème brûlée

La tarta
Pie

El flan (con caramelo)
Flan (with caramel)

La compota
Compote

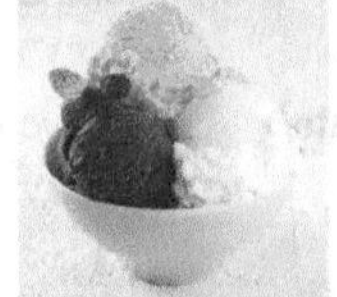

El helado
Ice cream

La nata montada
Whipped cream

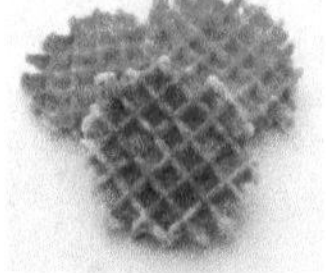

El gofre
Waffles

La tarta / el dulce
Cake

El buñuelo
Donut

Los postres

Desserts

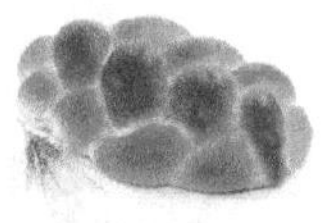

El bollo
Sweet bun

El arroz con leche
Rice pudding

La galleta
Cookie

El turrón
Nougat

Los churros
Churros with hot chocolate

El mantecado
Shortbread cookie

Las natillas
Custard

Las torrijas
French toast

Frases clave	Key phrases
¿Qué tienen de postre?	What do you have for dessert?
Me gustaría tres bolas de helado de vainilla con nata montada.	I would like three scoops of vanilla ice cream with whipped cream.

Los menús específicos : alérgicos, vegetarianos, niños

Specific menus: allergies, vegetarian, children's menus . . .

...-free diet
La dieta sin . . .

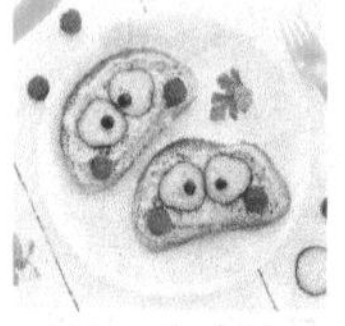

Children's menu
El menú infantil

Diabetic menu
Diabético

Frases clave	Key phrases
Estoy siguiendo una dieta sin sal / gluten / lactosa.	I follow a diet that is free of salt/gluten/lactose.
Sigo una dieta baja en grasas / en colesterol.	I follow a low-fat/low-cholesterol diet.
Soy alérgico(a) a los frutos secos / al huevo.	I'm allergic to nuts/eggs.
Soy vegetariano(a) / vegano(a).	I'm a vegetarian/vegan.
No como carne / cerdo.	I don't eat meat/pork.
No bebo alcohol.	I don't drink alcohol.
Solo como productos kosher / halal.	I only eat kosher/halal products.

Las bebidas sin alcohol

Alcohol-free beverages

El agua
Water

El agua con gas
Sparkling water

El agua mineral
Mineral water

La gaseosa
Soda

El zumo de frutas
Fruit juice

El sirope de menta
Alcohol-free mint julep

La limonada
Lemonade

El granizado
Slushie

Sin alcohol
Alcohol-free

El café
Coffee

El descafeinado
Decaffeinated coffee/decaf

El café con leche
Café au lait

Las bebidas sin alcohol

Alcohol-free beverages

El chocolate
(Hot) cocoa/ chocolate

El té
Tea

La infusión
Tea infusion

Frases clave	Key phrases
Tomaré agua.	I'll have water.
¿Tiene botellas de agua grandes?	Do you have large bottles of water?
Me gustaría un vaso de agua con hielo.	I would like a glass of ice water.

Las bebidas alcohólicas

Alcoholic beverages

La botella
Bottle

El vaso
Glass

El vino tinto
Red wine

El vino blanco
White wine

El vino rosado
Rosé wine

El cava
Cava (sparkling wine)

La cerveza
Beer

La caña
Small glass of beer

La sangría
Sangria

El anís
Pastis

El jerez
Sherry

El ron
Rum

Las bebidas alcohólicas

Alcoholic beverages

El champán
Champagne

El cóctel
Cocktail

El güisqui
Whisky

El coñac
Cognac

El vermú
Vermouth

El cubalibre
Rum and cola

Frases clave	Key phrases
¿Qué vino me aconseja para acompañar este plato?	What wine do you recommend to go with this dish?
¡Salud!	Cheers!
Para beber, voy a tomar . . .	I want . . . to drink.
¿Tiene vino por copas?	Do you have wine by the glass?

La cuenta

Paying the bill

Pagar
To pay

La tarjeta de crédito
Credit card

Un recibo
Receipt

El efectivo
Cash

La cuenta
Bill

El terminal con tarjeta de crédito
Credit card reader

La propina
Tip

La cuenta

Paying the bill

Frases clave	Key phrases
La cuenta, por favor.	The bill, please.
Queremos pagar a escote.	We would like to pay separately.
Voy a pagar en efectivo.	I am going to pay cash.
¿Puedo darme un recibo?	May I have a receipt?
Quédese con el cambio.	Keep the change.
¿Admiten las tarjetas de crédito?	Do you take credit cards?

¡Buenas noches!

Good night!

Las camas

Beds and bedrooms

La habitación doble
Double room

La habitación individual
Single room

La habitación familiar
Family room

La cama de matrimonio
Double bed

Las camas separadas
Twin beds

La cama supletoria
Extra bed

El colchón
Mattress

La manta
Pillow

La almohada
Blanket

La sábana
Sheet

Los tipos de alojamiento

Types of lodging

El hotel
Hotel

El apartahotel
Extended-stay hotel

La casa de huéspedes
Guest house

La casa rural
Cottage

El albergue juvenil
Youth hostel

La familia de acogida
Host family

El parador de turismo
State-run luxury hotel

El piso
Apartment

En una habitación de una casa particular
Room in a private house

El camping
Camping, campsite

Los tipos de alojamiento

Types of lodging

Frases clave	Key phrases
¿Qué precio tiene por noche?	How much is it per night?
¿El desayuno está incluido?	Is breakfast included?
¿Puedo ver la habitación?	May I see the room?
He reservado una habitación a nombre de . . .	I reserved a room under the name . . .

Suministros y servicios

Furnishings and services

El televisor
Television

El teléfono
Telephone

Internet
Internet

El aire acondicionado
Air conditioner

La caja fuerte
Safe

El wifi
Wi-Fi

El fax
Fax

La lavandería
Laundry

El garaje
Garage

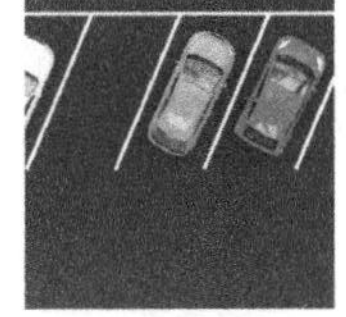

El aparcamiento
Parking

La piscina
Swimming pool

El hotel

Hotel

El hotel
Hotel

La recepción
Reception, front desk

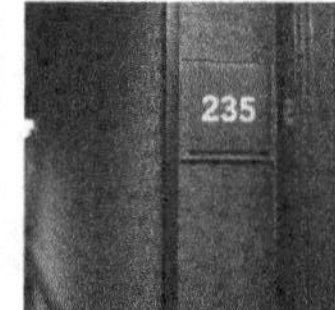

El número de habitación
Room number

La llave
Key

Las maletas
Luggage

La salida
Check-out

La propina
Tip

La media pensión
Half board

La pensión completa
Full board

El servicio de habitaciones
Room service

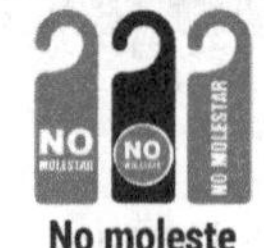

No moleste
Do not disturb

El hotel

Hotel

Frases clave	Key phrases
¿Tienen habitaciones libres?	Do you have a vacancy?
Pensamos quedarnos tres noches / dos semanas.	We are planning to stay for three nights/for two weeks.
¿Cuál es el precio de una habitación doble / individual?	How much is a double/ single room?
¿Puedo tener una habitación con vistas al mar?	Can I have a room with an ocean view?
¿El hotel es accesible a las personas con discapacidad?	Is the hotel handicap-accessible?

El camping
Camping

El camping
Camping, campsite

El remolque
Trailer

La autocaravana
Camper, motorhome

La tienda de campaña
Tent

El bungalow
Bungalow

El mobil home
Mobile home

La cabaña
Cabin

El saco de dormir
Sleeping bag

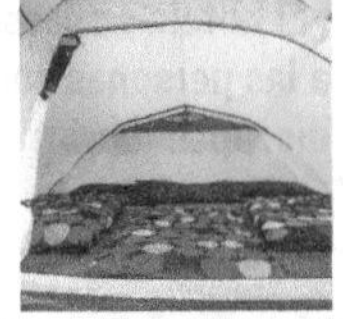

La colchoneta (aislante)
(Sleeping) mat

Los sanitarios, los aseos
Toilet facilities

Las duchas
Showers

La fogata
Campfire

El camping

Camping

El agua potable
Drinking water

La cantimplora
Canteen

El hornillo
Camp stove

La mochila
Backpack

La linterna
Flashlight

Los binoculares
Binoculars

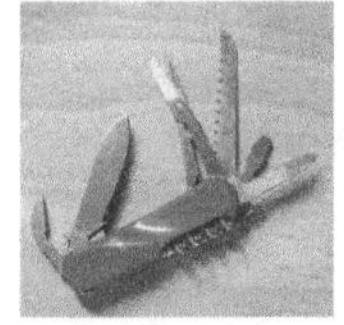

La navaja
Penknife, pocket knife

La nevera
Cooler

El camping
Camping

Frases clave	Key phrases
Querría el mismo lugar que el año pasado.	I would like the same place that I had last year.
¿Está permitada la acampada libre?	Is free camping allowed?
¿Hay alguna forma de dormir al raso?	Is it possible to sleep under the stars?

El apartamento

Apartment

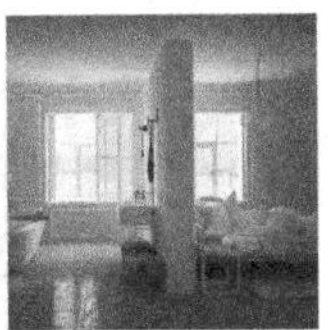

El apartamento
Apartment

La casa
House

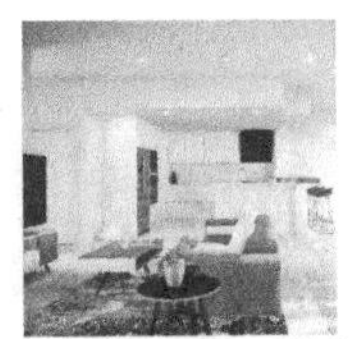

El apartamento amueblado
Furnished apartment

El dueño
Owner

El alquiler
Rental, rent

La fianza
(Security) deposit

El balcón
Balcony

La terraza
Terrace

El patio
Patio, yard

El piso
Floor (story)

La planta baja
Ground floor

El jardín
Garden, yard

El apartamento
Apartment

El televisor
Television

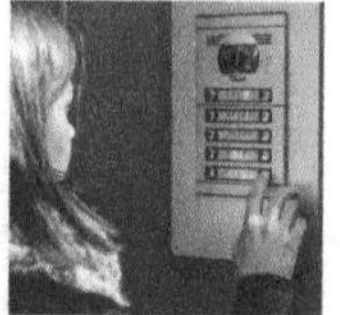

El telefonillo
Intercom

El ascensor
Elevator

La escalera
Stairs

El acceso para discapacitados
Handicap access

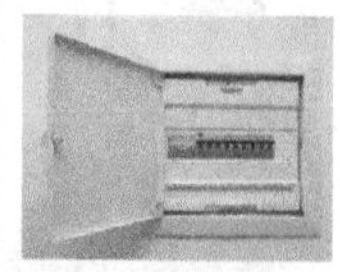

El contador eléctrico
Electric meter

La luz
Light

La calefacción
Heater

El cubo de la basura
Trash can

El lavavajillas
Dishwasher

La lavadora
Washer

La secadora
Dryer

El apartamento
Apartment

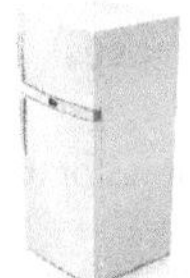

El frigorífico
Refrigerator

El horno
Oven

La aspiradora
Vacuum cleaner

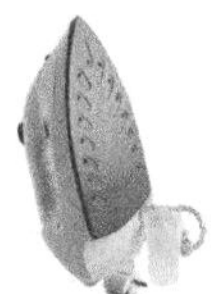

La plancha
Iron

La cocina
Kitchen

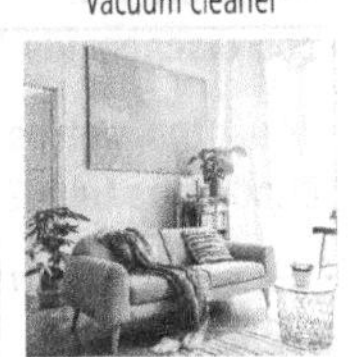

La sala de estar
Living room

El dormitorio
Bedroom

El cuarto de baño
Bathroom

El pasillo
Hall

El apartamento

Apartment

Frases clave	Key phrases
¿Cuál es la dirección del apartamento?	What is the address of the apartment?
¿El apartamento es accesible a las personas con discapacidad?	Is the apartment handicap-accessible?
¿Cuántos metros cuadrados tiene?	How many square meters is it?
¿Es un piso céntrico?	Is it in a central location?
Se alquila	For rent
Se vende	For sale
¿Proveen la ropa blanca (sábanas, fundas de almohadas, toallas, manteles, etcétera)?	Do you provide linen (sheets, pillowcases, towels, tablecloths, etc.)?
¿Dónde se tiran las bolsas de basura?	Where do you dispose of trash bags?
¿Cómo funciona el / la . . .?	How does the . . . work?
¿Cómo se sube / se baja la temperatura?	How do you raise/lower the temperature?

En el cuarto de baño

In the bathroom

El cuarto de baño
Bathroom

La ducha
Shower

La bañera
Bathtub

El lavabo
Bathroom sink, washbasin

El grifo
Faucet

El jabón
Soap

A alfombrilla de baño
Bath mat

El váter
Toilet

El papel higiénico
Toilet paper

El espejo
Mirror

El cepillo de dientes
Toothbrush

La pasta de dientes
Toothpaste

En el cuarto de baño

In the bathroom

El gel de ducha
Shower gel

El champú
Shampoo

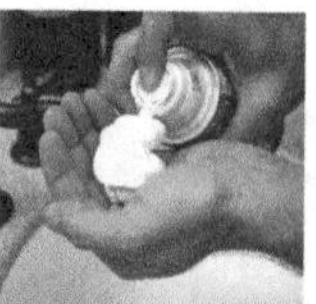

La crema de afeitar
Shaving cream

El gel
Gel

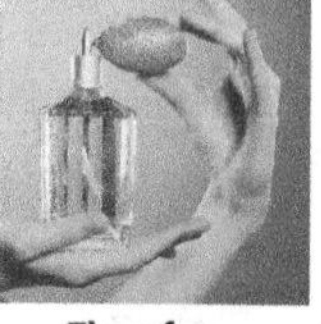

El perfume
Perfume

El desodorante
Deodorant

El secador de pelo
Hair dryer

La cuchilla
Razor

La afeitadora eléctrica
Electric razor/shaver

El peine
Comb

El cepillo
Brush

La toalla
Towel

En el cuarto de baño

In the bathroom

La toallita
Washcloth

Frases clave	Key phrases
¿Dónde está el baño?	Where's the bathroom?
No hay más papel higiénico.	There's no more toilet paper.
El lavabo está atascado.	The sink is clogged/stopped up.

¡Salgamos!

Outings

¿Cuánto cuesta?

How much is it?/How much does it cost?

El precio
Price

Comprar
To buy

Gratuito
Free

De pago
Paid (fee applies)

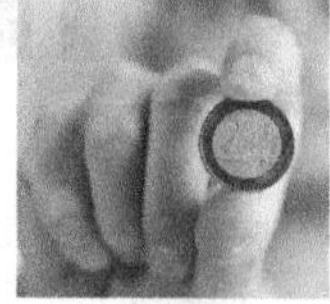

Barato
Cheap (inexpensive)

Caro
Expensive

Entrada libre
Free admission

Les rebajas
Discounts

¿Cuánto cuesta?

How much is it?/How much does it cost?

Frases clave	Key phrases
¿Cuánto cuesta?	How much does it cost?
¿Admiten tarjetas de crédito?	Do you take credit cards?
Quédese con la vuelta.	Keep the change.
¿Hay que pagar entrada?	Is there an admission fee?
¿Cobran por el servicio?	Is there a fee for the service?

El dinero
Money

El efectivo
Cash

La moneda
Coins

El billete
Bills, paper money

El euro
Euro

El céntimo
Cent, penny

La tarjeta de crédito
Credit card

El datáfono
Credit card reader

El código personal
PIN/Personal Identification Number

La firma
Signature

Pagar
To pay

El recibo
Receipt

El cajero automático
Automatic teller

El dinero

Money

El banco
Bank

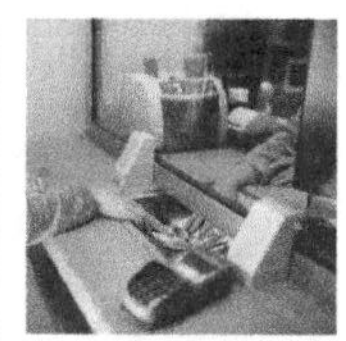

La oficina de cambio
Currency Exchange office

Frases clave	Key phrases
Tengo suelto.	I have change.
¿Llevas dinero?	Do you have any money on you?
¿Tienes una moneda de un euro?	Do you have a one-euro coin?
¿Me prestas veinte euros?	Can you lend me twenty euros?
Querría pagar con tarjeta.	I'd like to pay with a credit card.
Quiero sacar dinero.	I want to withdraw money.
Estoy buscando un cajero automático.	I am looking for an automatic teller.
Introduzca su tarjeta, por favor.	Please insert your card.
El cajero se me ha tragado la tarjeta.	The cash machine seized my card.
Vengo a sacar dinero de mi cuenta.	I came to withdraw money from my account.
¿Me lo puede dar en billetes pequeños?	May I please have small bills?
Quiero cambiar dólar americano a pesos mexicanos	I would like to exchange dollars for Mexican pesos.

Las tiendas

Stores and shops

Abierto
Open

Cerrado
Closed

La salida
Entrance

La entrada
Exit

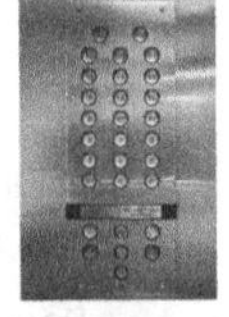

El ascensor
Elevator

La escalera
Stairs

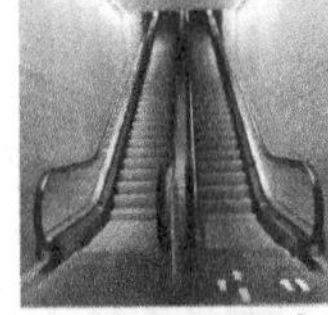

Las escaleras mecánicas
Escalator

El acceso para discapacitados
Handicap access

La tienda de alimentación
Grocery store

La frutería y verdulería
Produce market

La panadería
Bakery

La pastelería
Bakery (pastry shop)

Las tiendas

Stores and shops

La carnicería
Butcher shop

La pescadería
Fish market/fish section

La bodega
Liquor store

La zapatería
Shoe store

La tienda de ropa
Clothing store

La librería
Bookstore

El estanco
Tobacconist's shop/smoke shop

La tintorería
Dry cleaner

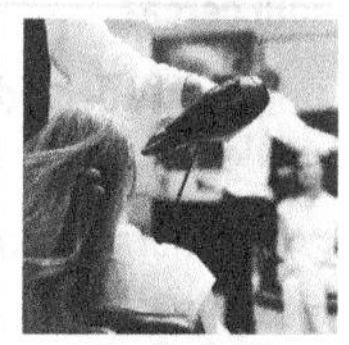

La peluquería
Hair salon, hairdresser

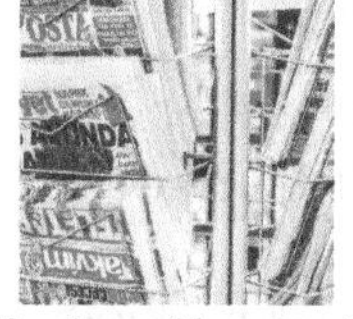

El quiosco (de prensa)
Newsstand

El mercado
Market

El gran almacén
Department store

El supermercado

Stores and shops

El probador
Fitting room

Frases clave	Key phrases
¿En qué zona están las tiendas?	What area are the stores in?/Where's the shopping district?
¿Hay alguna panadería por aquí cerca?	Is there a bakery around here?
¿Me puede decir dónde venden . . . ?	Can you tell me where they sell . . . ?
¿A qué hora abren / cierran las tiendas?	When do the stores open/close?
¿Dónde está la sección de caballero / señora / niño?	Where is the men's/women's/children's department?
¿Hay algún mercado?	Is there a market?
¿Qué días hay mercado?	On what days is the market open?
Eso es todo, gracias.	That will be all, thank you.

El supermercado
Supermarket

El supermercado
Supermarket

El carrito de la compra
Grocery/shopping cart

La cesta (de la compra)
(Shopping) basket

La sección
Department

El precio
Price

La caja
Checkout

El cajero
Cashier, clerk

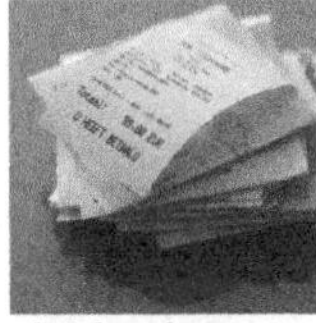

El ticket de compra
Receipt

La bolsa
(Grocery) bag

El pan y los pasteles
Bread and pastries

El queso
Cheese

Las verduras
Vegetables

El supermercado

Supermarket

El pescado

Fish

La carne

Meat

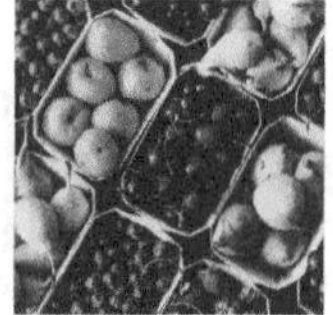

Las frutas

Fruits

Las bebidas

Beverages, drinks

Las bebidas alcohólicas

Alcoholic beverages

Los recuerdos y la artesanía

Souvenirs and crafts

El regalo
Gift

El recuerdo
Souvenir

El imán de nevera
(Refrigerator) magnet

La postal
Postcard

El papel de regalo
Wrapping paper

El abanico
Fan

Las castañuelas
Castanets

La muñeca
Doll

El turrón
Nougat

El jamón
Ham

La cerámica
Ceramics, pottery

El encaje
Lace

Los recuerdos y la artesanía

Souvenirs and crafts

El cuero
Leather

Frases clave	Key phrases
¿Cuáles son los productos típicos de aquí?	What products are typical of this region?
¿Hay alguna especialidad local?	Is there a local specialty?
¿Qué tienen de realmente típico?	What do you have that is truly typical (of the region)?
Estoy buscando un regalo fácil de llevar de viaje.	I am looking for a gift that is easy to transport.
¿Me lo puede envolver para regalo?	Can you gift wrap it for me?

La ropa
Clothes

El eslip
Briefs

Las bragas
Panties

Los calzoncillos
Boxer shorts

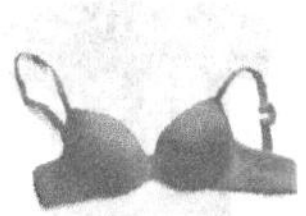

El sujetador
Bra

Los pantis
Stockings

El pijama
Pajamas

El camisón
Nightgown

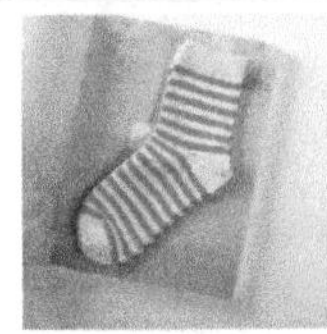

El calcetín
Sock

La camiseta
Undershirt

El vestido
Dress

La falda
Skirt

La blusa
Blouse

La ropa

Clothes

El suéter
Sweater (pullover)

La chaqueta
Jacket

Los pantalones
Pants

Los vaqueros, los tejanos
Jeans

Los pantalones cortos
Shorts

La camiseta
T-shirt

El traje
Suit

La camisa
Shirt

El chándal
Sweatpants

La cazadora
Jacket

El chubasquero
Raincoat

El abrigo
Coat

La ropa

Clothes

La seda
Silk

La lana
Wool

El algodón
Cotton

El lino
Linen

El cuero
Leather

El terciopelo
Velvet

De rayas
Striped

A cuadros
Plaid, checkered

Floreado
Floral

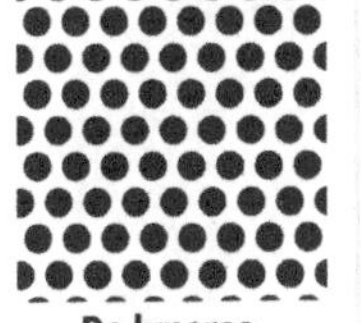

De lunares
Polka dotted

Liso
Plain (not patterned)

Negro
Black

La ropa

Clothes

Blanco
White

Rojo
Red

Verde
Green

Gris
Gray

Marrón
Brown

Amarillo
Yellow

Azul
Blue

Naranja
Orange

Rosa
Pink

Morado
Purple

La ropa

Clothes

Frases clave	Key phrases
Me gustaría ver el / la que está en el escaparate.	I would like to see the one in the window/showcase.
¿Cómo me queda?	How does it fit/look?
Me queda demasiado corto / ancho.	It's too small/big.
¿Lo / La tiene en la talla . . . ?	Do you have it in size . . . ?
¿Lo / La tiene en otro color?	Do you have it in another color?
Me gustaría probar este modelo.	I would like to try this style.
Estos pantalones no me caben.	These pants don't fit me.
Me gustaría comprar ropa interior.	I would like to buy some underwear.
¿Se puede lavar a máquina?	Is it machine washable?
Si hay algún problema, ¿lo puedo cambiar?	Can I exchange it if it isn't right?

El calzado

Footwear

El zapato
Shoe

La bota
Boot

La bota de lluvia
Rain boot

El botín
Ankle boot

Las deportivas
Sneaker

El escarpín
Pump

El zapato de tacón
High-heeled shoe

El mocasín
Moccasin

La sandalia
Sandal

La chancleta
Flip-flop

La alpargata
Espadrille, canvas shoe

La zapatilla
Slipper

El calzado
Footwear

La bota de montaña
Hiking boot

El cordón
Shoelace

La suela
Sole

Frases clave	Key phrases
Quiero un par de zapatos / sandalias / deportivas.	I would like a pair of shoes/ sandals/sneakers.
Calzo un 40.	I wear a size 40 shoe.
¿Me los puedo probar?	May I try them on?
Me gustaría zapatos planos.	I would like flat shoes.

Los accesorios y las joyas

Accessories and jewelry

El guante
Glove

El gorro
Wool hat

La bufanda
Scarf

El sombrero
Hat

El cinturón
Belt

La corbata
Necktie

La mochila
Backpack

El bolso
Handbag, purse

La cartera
Wallet

El monedero
Wallet, change purse

Las gafas de sol
Sunglasses

La gorra
Cap

Los accesorios y las joyas

Accessories and jewelry

El paraguas
Umbrella

El reloj
Watch

El anillo
Ring

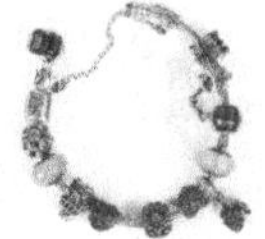

La pulsera
Bracelet

El collar
Necklace

El pendiente
Earring

El colgante
Pendant

Al aire libre

Outdoors

La montaña
Mountain

El esquí (alpino / de fondo)
Skiing (alpine/ cross-country)

El trineo
Sled

El snowboard
Snowboard

Las raquetas de nieve
Snowshoes

El guía de montaña
Mountain guide

La nieve
Snow

El teleférico
Cable car/cableway

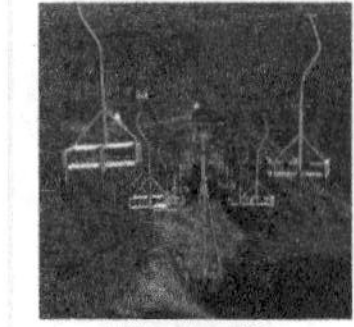

El telesilla
Chairlift

Los remontes
Ski lifts

La bota de montaña
Hiking shoe/boot

El alpinismo, el montañismo
Mountain climbing

Al aire libre

Outdoors

El refugio
Shelter, mountain cottage

La cuerda
Rope

La escalada
(Rock) climbing

El senderismo
Hiking

El mapa
Map

El camino
Trail

El ciclismo
Cycling

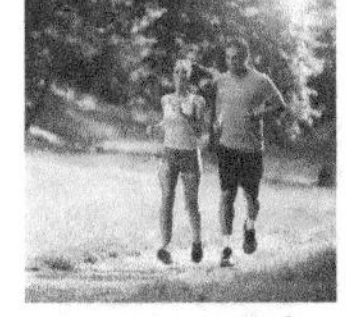

La carrera a pie
Running

El parapente
Paragliding

El paracaidismo
Parachuting/
skydiving

El canotaje
Canoeing

La pesca
Fishing

Al aire libre

Outdoors

La vela
Yachting

El surf
Surfing

La equitación
(Horseback) riding

El golf
Golf

El fútbol
Soccer

El campo
Soccer field

El balón, la pelota
Ball

El equipo
Team

El partido
Game, match

El medio tiempo
Half-time

El árbitro
Referee

El rugby
Rugby

Al aire libre

Outdoors

El estadio
Stadium

El atletismo
Track and field

El tenis
Tennis

La pelota
Tennis ball

La cancha de tenis
Tennis court

La raqueta
(Tennis) racket

La red
Net

Frases clave	Key phrases
Juego al tenis.	I play tennis.
Los miércoles tengo clase de golf.	I have golf lessons on Wednesdays.

De interior

Indoors

El gimnasio
Gym

El yoga
Yoga

El judo
Judo

El voleibol
Volleyball

El baloncesto
Basketball

El balonmano
Handball

El bádminton
Badminton

La gimnasia
Gymnastics

El tenis de mesa
Table tennis, ping-pong

La natación
Swimming

La esgrima
Fencing

En la playa

At the beach

La playa
Beach

La arena
Sand

El mar
Ocean, sea

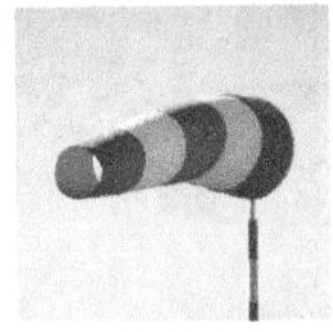

La costa, el litoral
Shore, coast

El acantilado
Cliff

El viento
Wind

La ola
Wave

La marea (alta / baja)
(High/low) tide

El faro
Lighthouse

El puerto
Port, harbor

El bañador de una pieza
One-piece bathing suit

El bañador
Bathing suit, swim trunks

En la playa

At the beach

El bikini
Bikini

La gorra
Cap

La crema solar
Sunscreen, suntan lotion

Las gafas de sol
Sunglasses

El sombrero
Hat

Las chanclas
Flip-flops

La toalla
Towel

La sombrilla, el parasol
(Beach) umbrella, parasol

El flotador
Tube, float

La bandera
Flag

Les gafas de buceo
Diving mask

La aleta
Flipper, swim fin

En la playa
At the beach

La ducha
Shower

El buceo, el submarinismo
(Scuba) diving

El cubo
Bucket

La pala
Shovel

El rastrillo
Rake

La vela
Yachting

El patín (de pedales)
Pedal boat

El windsurf
Windsurfing

En la playa

At the beach

Frases clave	Key phrases
¿Cuál es el mejor lugar para pescar / hacer submarinismo?	What is the best place to fish/ to dive?
¿Hay un club de vela por aquí?	Is there a yacht club around here?
¿A qué distancia está el mar?	How far away is the ocean?
¿Dónde está la playa?	Where's the beach?
¿Dónde está el puesto de seguridad?	Where is the lifeguard station?
¿Sabe si hay una playa naturista / vigilada por aquí?	Do you know if there is a nudist beach/beach with supervised swimming around here?
¿(El agua) cubre aquí?	Can you touch the bottom here?/Is it shallow here?
¿A qué hora sube / baja la marea?	When is high/low tide?
¿Hay medusas / erizos?	Are there any jellyfish/sea urchins?
¿Me puede cuidar las cosas mientras voy al agua?	Can you watch my things while I go for a swim?
¿Está permitido bañarse aquí?	Is swimming allowed here?

En la piscina

At the swimming pool

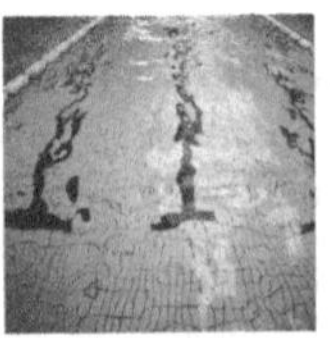

La piscina
Swimming pool

Las gafas de natación
Goggles

El gorro de baño
Bathing cap

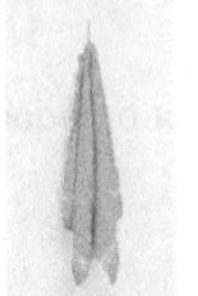

La toalla
Towel

La tabla
Kickboard

La aleta
Flipper, swim fin

El socorrista
Lifeguard

La ducha
Shower

En la piscina

At the swimming pool

Frases clave	Key phrases
No sé nadar.	I don't know how to swim.
¿Dónde está la piscina más cercana?	Where is the nearest swimming pool?
¿Cuáles son los horarios de la piscina?	When is the pool open?
¿Es una piscina al aire libre o una piscina cubierta?	Is it an outdoor or indoor pool?

El cine

The movies

El cine
The movies/movie theater

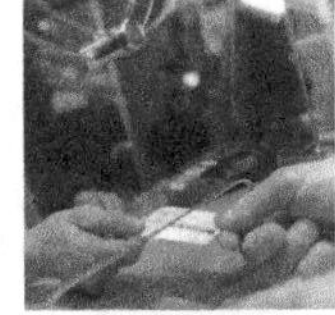

La taquilla
Ticket window

El asiento
Seat

La película
Movie

La sesión
Show

El billete
Admission ticket

Frases clave	Key phrases
¿A qué hora empieza / termina la sesión?	When does the show start/ end?
¿Cuánto (tiempo) dura la película?	How long does the movie last?
¿La película es en versión original y está subtitulada en inglés?	Is the movie the original version, with English subtitles?
¿La película sigue en cartelera?	Is the movie still playing?

El teatro
Theater

El teatro
Theater

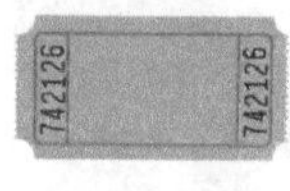

La entrada
Admission ticket

La obra
Play

El actor
Actor

La actriz
Actress

El asiento
Seat

El entreacto
Intermission

La danza
Dance/dancing

El ballet
Ballet

El bailarín
(Male) dancer

La bailarina
(Female) dancer, ballerina

La música
Music

La ópera
Opera

La música clásica
Classical music

La comedia musical
Musical

El tablao
Flamenco venue

El flamenco
Flamenco

El director de orquesta
Conductor

La orquesta
Orchestra

El cantante
Singer, vocalist

El músico
Musician

La zarzuela
Operetta

El concierto
Concert

La sala
Performance hall

Salir

La música

Music

El escenario
Stage

La canción
Song

La flauta
Flute

La guitarra acústica
Acoustic guitar

La guitarra eléctrica
Electric guitar

El piano
Piano

El violín
Violin

La batería
Drum set

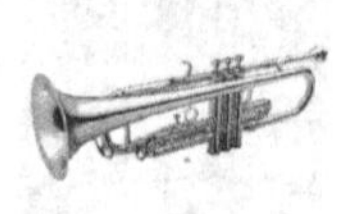

La trompeta
Trumpet

El saxofón
Saxophone

El acordeón
Accordion

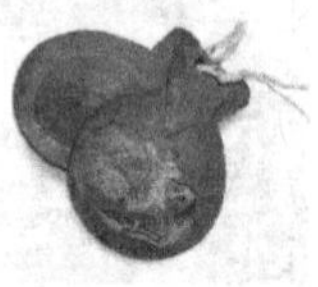

Las castañuelas
Castanets

La música

Music

La pandereta
Tambourine

Las palmas
Handclapping

Frases clave	Key phrases
¿Quedan entradas para la función de esta noche?	Can you still get tickets for tonight's performance?
¿Tiene entradas para otro día?	Can you get tickets for another day?
¿A qué hora empieza?	When/what time does it start?
Me gustaría comprar billetes para el espectáculo de danza clásica / contemporánea / folclórica.	I would like to buy tickets for the classical/ contemporary/folk dance performance.
¿Dónde tiene lugar el festival de rock / pop / rap / jazz?	Where is the rock/pop/rap/ jazz festival?
¿Tiene un programa o una guía de espectáculos?	Do you have a program or guide to the shows?

El museo
Museum

El museo
Museum

El arte
Art

La pinacoteca
Gallery

El museo de historia natural
Natural history museum

La exposición
Exhibit

La escultura
Sculpture

El pintar
To paint

La pintura
Painting

El dibujo
Drawing

La cerámica
Ceramics, pottery

La fotografía
Photography

El museo

Museum

Frases clave	Key phrases
¿A qué hora abre / cierra el museo?	What time does the museum open/close?
¿Dónde está el museo de bellas artes?	Where is the museum of fine arts?
¿En qué sala está el *Guernica*?	Which room is *Guernica* in?
¿Cuál es el sentido de la visita?	What is the sequence of the tour/visit?
¿Se pueden sacar fotos?	Can you take pictures/ photos?
¿Hacen descuentos para niños / estudiantes / personas mayores / familias numerosas / grupos?	Are there discounts for children/students/seniors/ large families/groups?
¿Dónde está la consigna / el guardarropa?	Where is the locker room/ the cloakroom?

Las salidas y las fiestas

Outings and celebrations

La fiesta
Party, celebration

El bar
Bar

La discoteca
Discotheque

La feria
Fair

El desfile
Parade

La verbena
Dance party

El espectáculo piromusical
Musical fireworks display

La corrida
Bullfight

El torero
Bull fighter

La plaza (de toros)
Arena

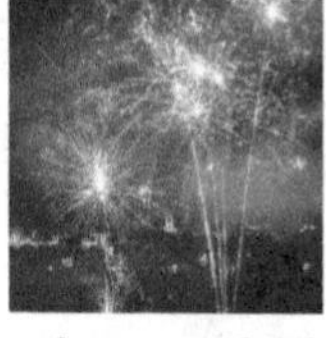

Los fuegos artificiales
Fireworks

El cumpleaños
Birthday

Las salidas y las fiestas

Outings and celebrations

Frases clave	Key phrases
¿Qué se puede hacer aquí por las noches?	What is there to do at night around here?
¿A qué hora / Dónde quedamos?	When/where will we meet?
¿Vamos a tomar algo?	Shall we have a drink?
¿Qué tenéis pensado hacer esta noche / mañana?	What are your plans for tonight/tomorrow?
¿Dónde está la zona de los bares?	Where is the bar district?
¿Cuáles son los lugares de moda?	Where are the hot spots?
¿Dónde se puede ir a bailar?	Where can you go dancing?
¿Qué tipo de música ponen?	What kind of music do they play?
¿La entrada incluye una consumición?	Is a drink included with the cover charge?
¿Qué se celebra?	What are you celebrating?
¡Feliz cumpleaños!	Happy birthday!

¡Cuidado!

Caution!

El cuerpo

The body

La cabeza
Head

El cráneo
Skull

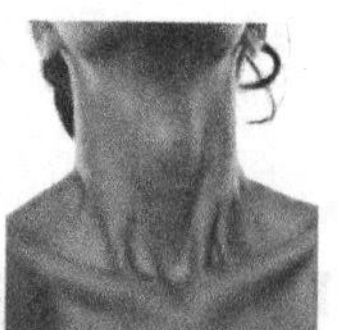

El cuello
Neck

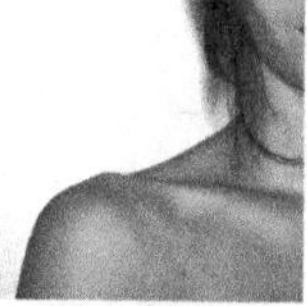

El hombro
Shoulder

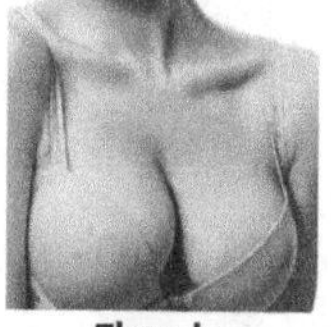

El pecho
Chest, breast

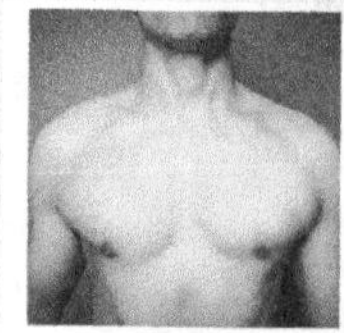

El torso
Torso

El brazo
Arm

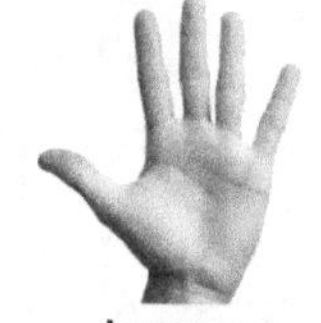

La mano
Hand

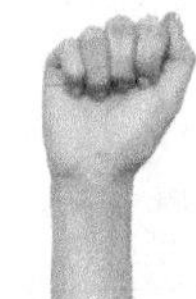

La muñeca
Wrist

El dedo
Finger

El pulgar
Thumb

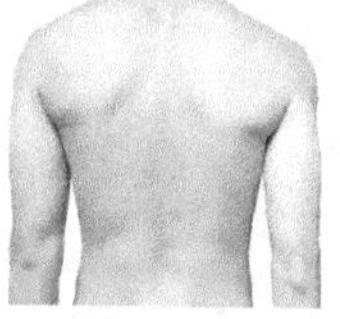

La espalda
Back

El cuerpo

The body

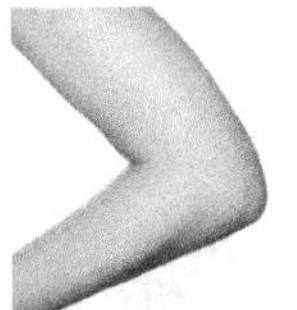

El codo
Elbow

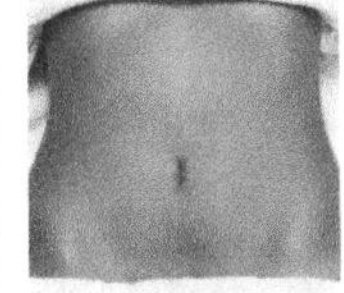

La barriga
Belly

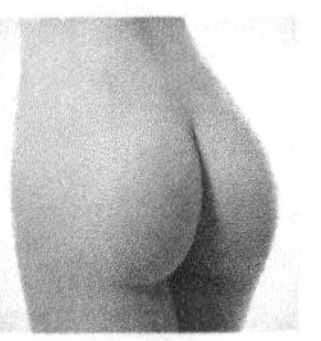

El trasero
Buttocks/bottom

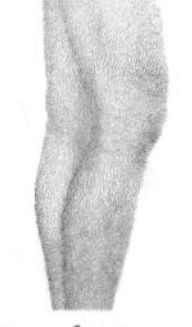

La pierna
Leg

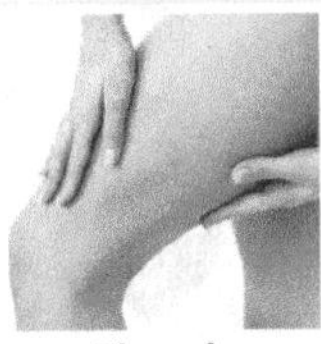

El muslo
Thigh

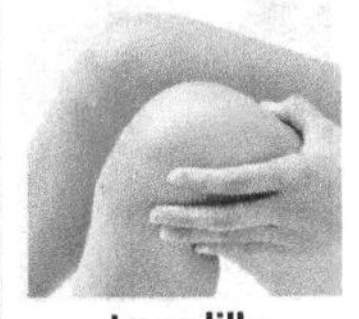

La rodilla
Knee

El tobillo
Ankle

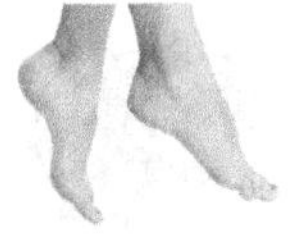

El pie
Feet

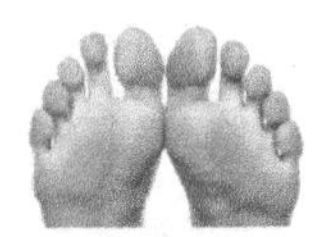

El dedo del pie
Toes

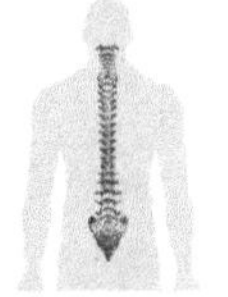

La columna vertebral
Spine, backbone

El músculo
Muscle

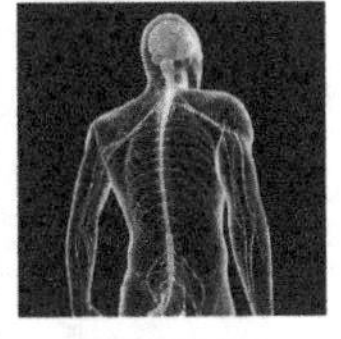

El nervio
Nerve

El cuerpo
The body

El hueso
Bone

La piel
Skin

La sangre
Blood

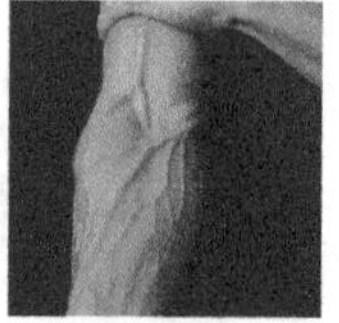

La vena
Vein

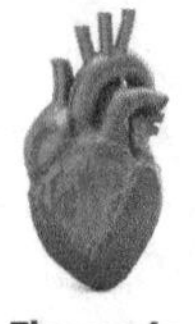

El corazón
Heart

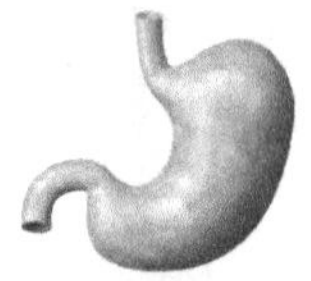

El estómago
Stomach

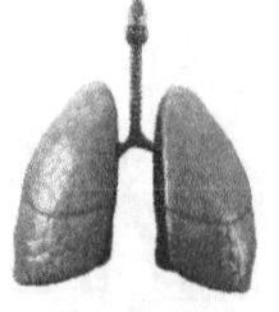

El pulmón
Lung

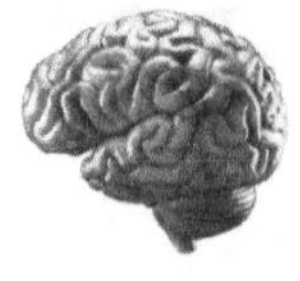

El cerebro
Brain

El hígado
Liver

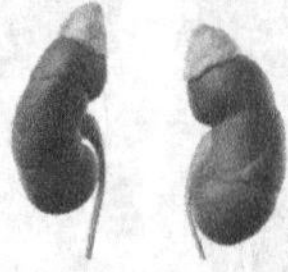

El riñón
Kidney

La cabeza
The head

La cara
Face

El pelo
Hair

Pelirrojo/moreno/ rubio
Redhead/brunette/ blonde

Calvo
Bald

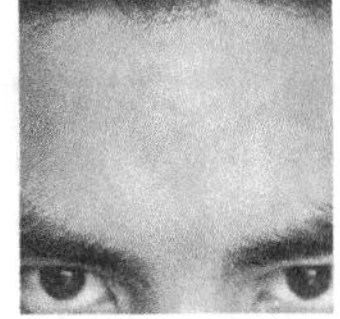

La frente
Forehead

El ojo
Eye

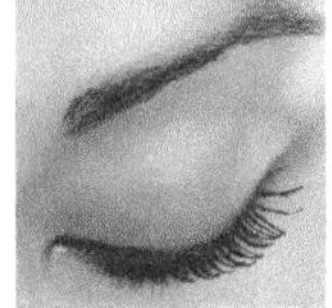

El párpado
Eyelid

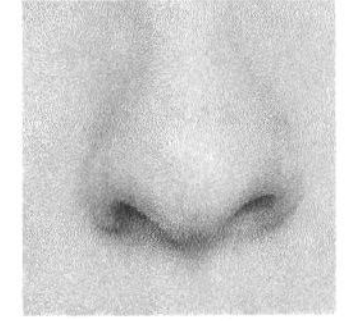

La nariz
Nose

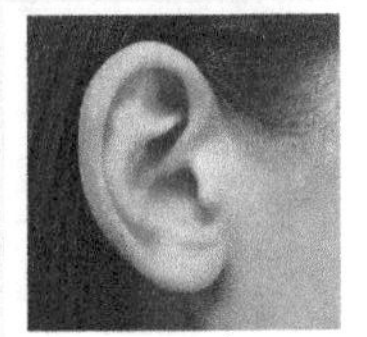

La oreja
Ear

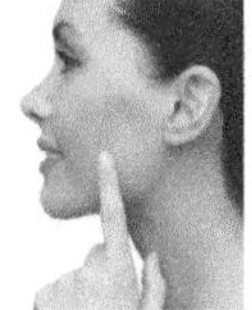

La mejilla
Cheek

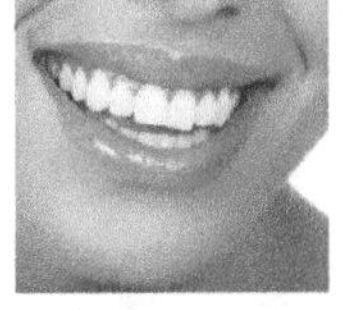

La boca
Mouth

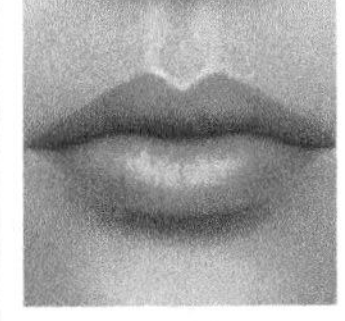

El labio
Lip

La cabeza

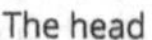

The head

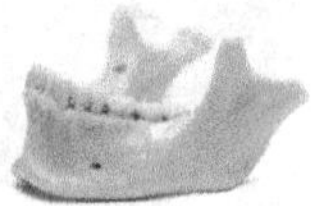

La mandíbula
Jaw

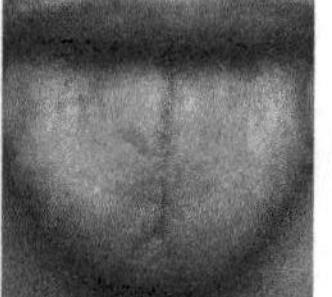

La lengua
Tongue

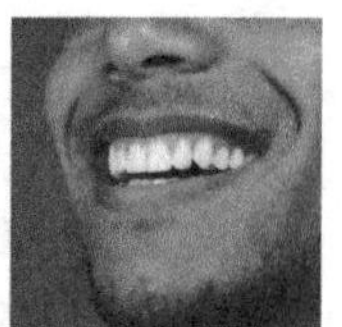

El diente
Teeth

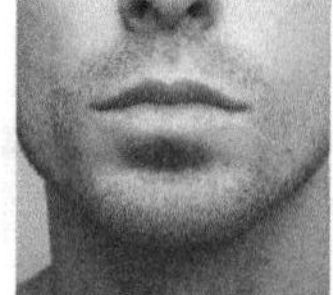

La barbilla
Chin

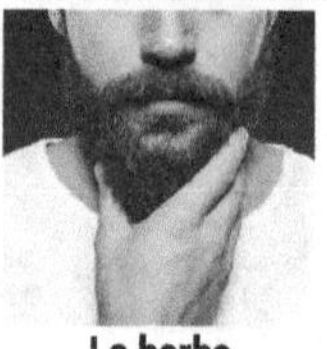

La barba
Beard

El bigote
Moustache

Las gafas
Glasses

Los médicos
Doctors

La consulta médica
Medical practice/ doctor's office

El médico de cabecera
General practitioner

El especialista
Specialist

El oculista
Ophthalmologist/ eye doctor

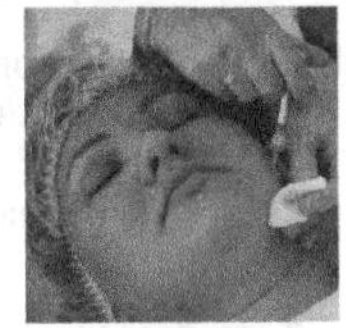

El dermatólogo
Dermatologist

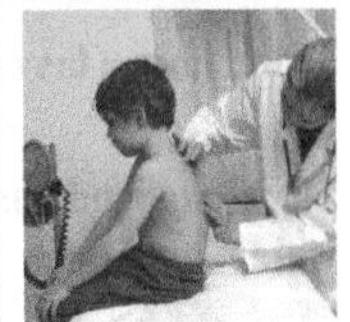

El pediatra
Pediatrician

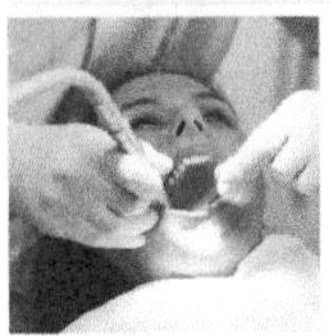

El dentista
Dentist

La enfermedad
Disease/illness

La receta
Prescription

Los médicos

Doctors

Frases clave	Key phrases
¿Me puede hacer una factura para el seguro médico?	Can you give me a receipt/ a copy of the bill for the health insurance company?
Me gustaría pedir hora.	I would like to make an appointment.
Tengo hora a las cuatro.	I have an appointment at four o'clock.
Estoy siguiendo un tratamiento para . . .	I am being treated for . . .
¿Es grave / contagioso?	Is it serious/contagious?

Los pacientes y los síntomas

Patients and their symptoms

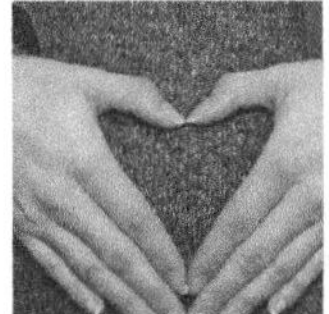

Embarazada
Pregnant

Diabético
Diabetic

Epiléptico
Epileptic

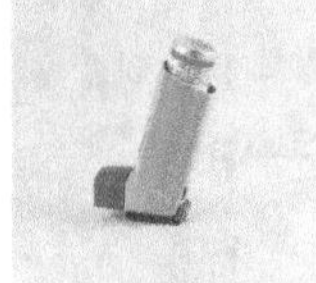

Asmático
Asthmatic

Alérgico
Allergic

La náusea
Nausea

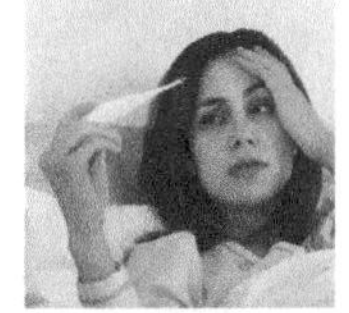

La fiebre
Fever

La tos
Cough

El catarro, el resfriado, el congestionado
(Head) cold

El dolor
Pain

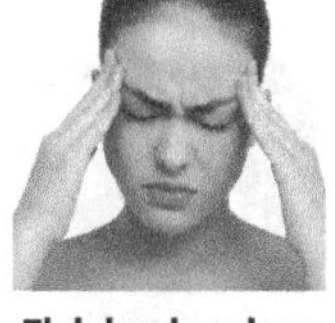

El dolor de cabeza
Headache

El dolor de garganta
Sore throat

Los pacientes y los síntomas

Patients and their symptoms

El dolor de muelas
Toothache

El dolor de espalda
Backache

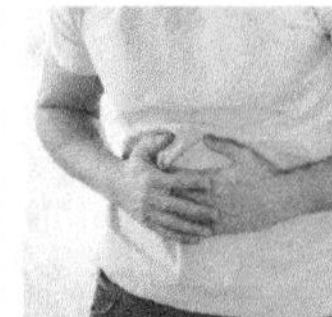

La acidez de estómago
Heartburn

La herida
Wound/injury

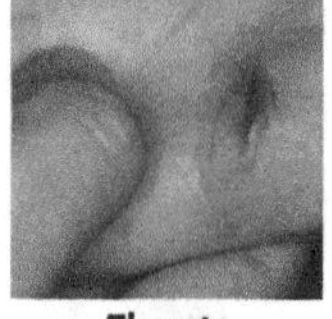

El corte
Cut

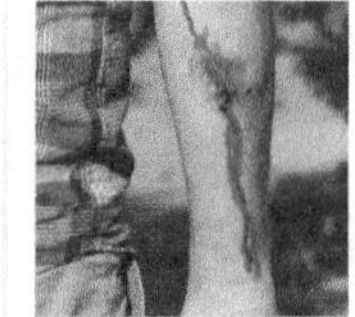

El sangrado
Bleeding

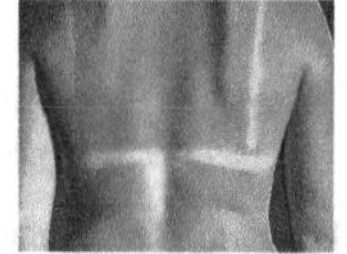

La quemadura
(Sun)burn

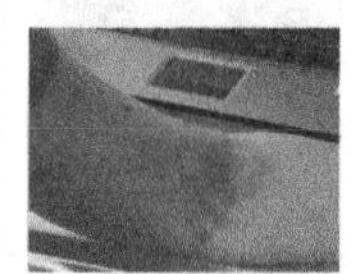

La erupción cutánea
Skin rash

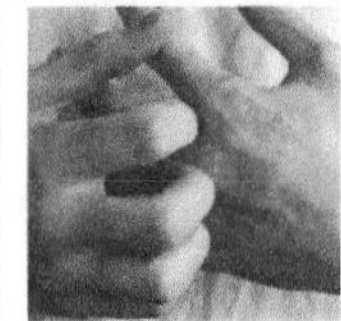

El picor
Itching

La diarrea
Diarrhea

Vomitar
To vomit

El cardenal, el moratón
Bruise

Los pacientes y los síntomas

Patients and their symptoms

Frases clave	Key phrases
Me duelen los pies.	My feet hurt.
Estoy enfermo.	I'm sick.
Me siento mal.	I do not feel well./I feel bad.
Tengo dolor de cabeza. / Me duele la cabeza.	I have a headache./My head hurts.
Me duele aquí / todo.	It hurts here/everywhere.
Me he dado un golpe.	I hurt/bumped myself.
Me he caído.	I fell.
Me he cortado.	I cut myself.
Me he torcido el tobillo.	I twisted/sprained my ankle.
Me ha picado una medusa.	I got stung by a jellyfish.
Me sangra la nariz.	I have a nosebleed./My nose is bleeding.
Tengo tortícolis.	I have a stiff neck.
Tengo náuseas.	I feel nauseous.
Me he quemado con el sol.	I got sunburned.
Me ha entrado algo en el ojo.	I've got something in my eye.
Estoy embarazada de . . . meses.	I am . . . months pregnant.

La farmacia y los medicamentos

Pharmacy and medicines

La farmacia
Pharmacy/drugstore

El farmacéutico
Pharmacist

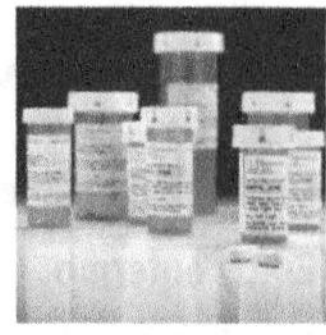

El medicamento
Medicine/medication

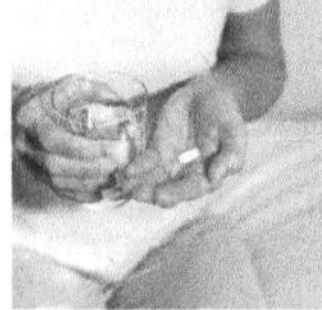

El calmante
Analgesic/painkiller

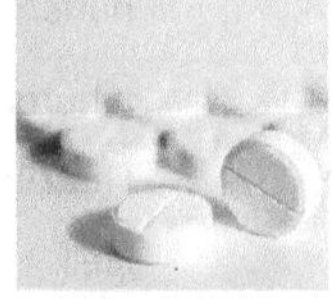

El comprimido
Tablet

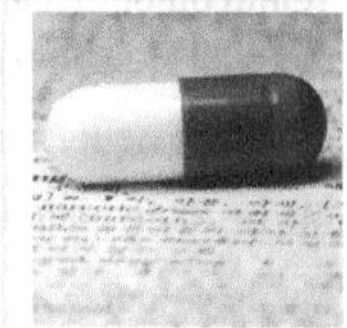

La pastilla
Capsule

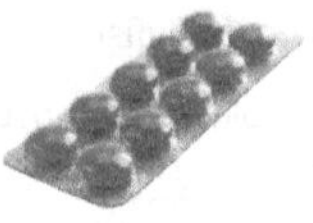

El antibiótico
Antibiotic

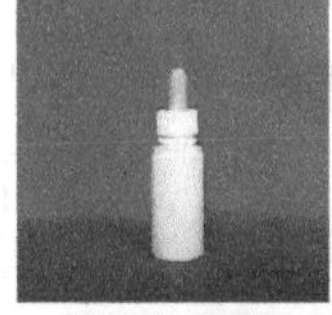

El antiséptico
Antiseptic

El termómetro
Thermometer

El jarabe para la tos
Cough syrup

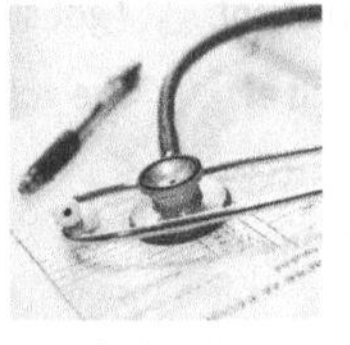

La receta
Prescription

El preservativo
Condom

La farmacia y los medicamentos

Pharmacy and medicines

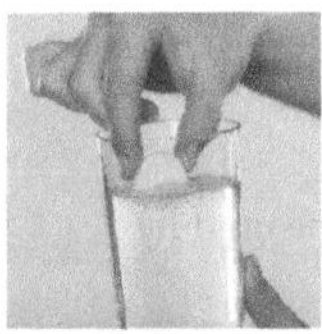

La aspirina®
Aspirin

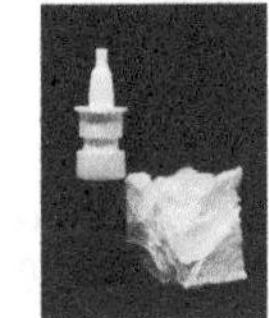

Las gotas para la nariz
Nose drops

El esparadrapo
(Medical) adhesive tape

La tirita®
Band-Aid™

La pomada
Ointment/salve

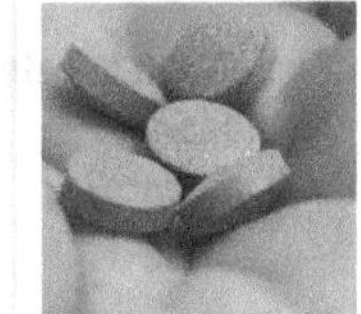

El somnífero
Sleeping pill

El laxante
Laxative

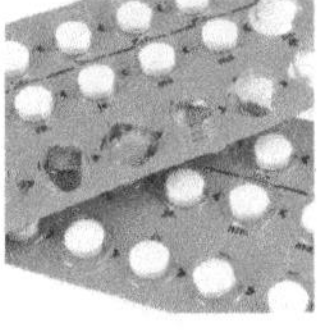

La píldora
Pill

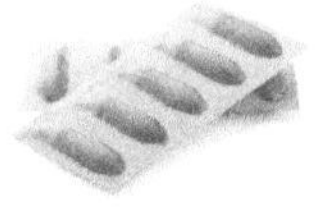

El supositorio
Suppository

La farmacia y los medicamentos

Pharmacy and medicines

Frases clave	Key phrases
¿Dónde está la farmacia de guardia?	Where is the on-duty pharmacy?
¿Tiene algo para la tos / la diarrea?	Do you have something for a cough/diarrhea?
¿Cuáles son los efectos secundarios del medicamento?	What are the side effects of the medicine?

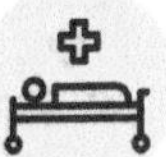

El hospital

Hospital

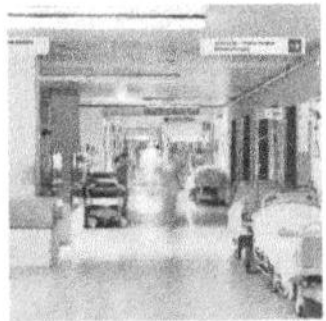

El hospital
Hospital

La clínica
Clinic

Las urgencias
Emergency room

La ambulancia
Ambulance

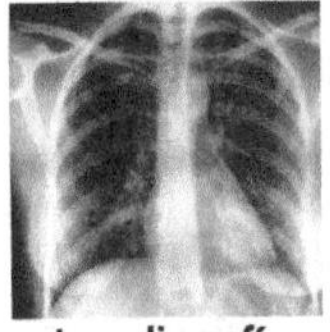

La radiografía
X-ray

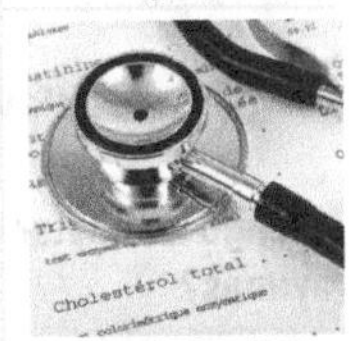

Los análisis clínicos
Medical analyses/tests

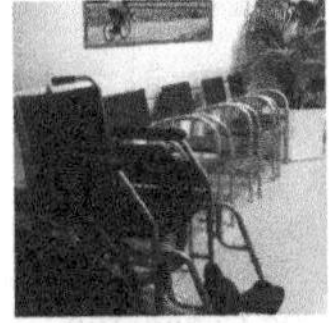

La sala de espera
Waiting room

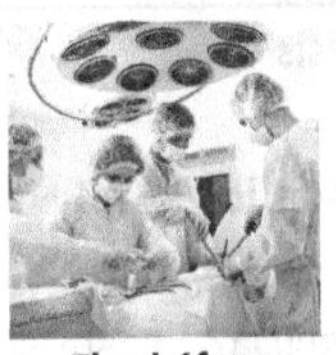

El quirófano
Operating room

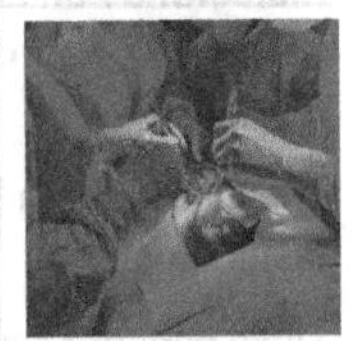

La operación
Operation

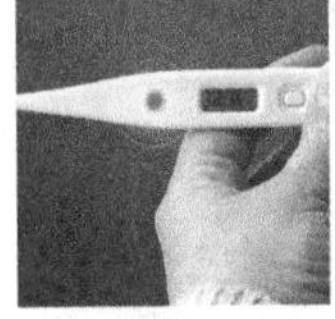

La temperatura
Temperature

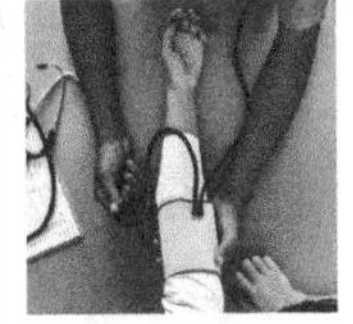

La tensión
Blood pressure

El examen médico
Medical exam

El hospital

Hospital

El cirujano
Surgeon

El enfermero
Nurse

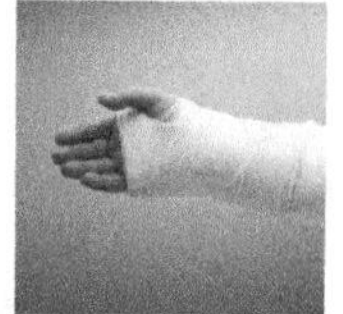

El yeso
Cast

Frases clave	Key phrases
¿Tengo que estar en ayunas?	Do I need to fast?
Vengo a hacer una radiografía / un análisis de sangre / un análisis de orina.	I'm here to get an X-ray/a blood analysis/a urine analysis.
¿Cuándo estarán listos los resultados?	When will the results be ready?
¿Va a ponerme anestesia?	Are you going to give me anesthesia?
Me han operado de . . .	I had surgery for . . .

La policía, la guardia civil y los bomberos

The police, the civil guard and the fire department

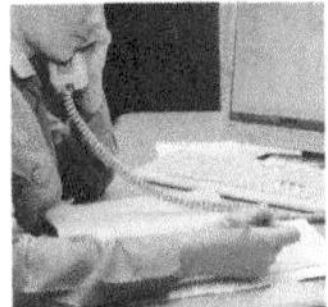

La comisaría de policía
Police station

El policía
Policeman

El parque de bomberos
Firehouse

El bombero
Fireman/firefighter

La guardia civil
Civil guard

El robo
Theft, robbery

El dinero
Money

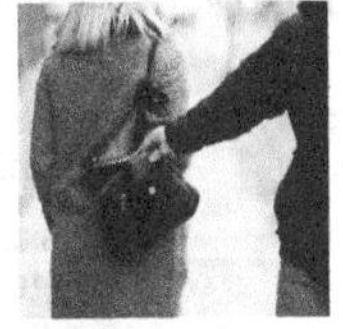

El carterista
Pickpocket

El pasaporte
Passport

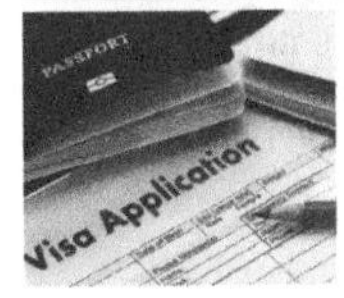

El visado turístico / de trabajo
Tourist/work visa

Herido
Injured, wounded

El incendio
Fire

La policía, la guardia civil y los bomberos

The police, the civil guard and the fire department

Frases clave	Key phrases
¡Socorro!	Help!
¡Auxilio!	Help!
¡Cuidado!	Watch out!
¡Fuego!	Fire!
Llamen a una ambulancia / a un médico / a la policía / a los bomberos.	Call an ambulance/a doctor/the police/the fire department.
¡Rápido!	Hurry!
¡Ayúdenme!	Help me!
¿Qué tengo que hacer?	What must I do?/What do I have to do?
Tengo que ponerme en contacto con el Consulado de los Estados Unidos.	I need to contact the U.S. consulate.
¿Dónde está la comisaría más cercana?	Where is the nearest police station?
Me han agredido.	I was assaulted/I got mugged.
Quiero poner una denuncia por robo.	I want to report a theft/ robbery.
Me han forzado el maletero / la puerta del coche y me han robado todo lo que tenía dentro.	Someone jimmied the trunk/the door of my car and stole everything in it.

La policía, la guardia civil y los bomberos

The police, the civil guard and the fire department

Frases clave	Key phrases
Me han robado la cartera / el bolso.	My wallet/handbag was stolen.
Había dinero y el pasaporte.	It contained my money and my passport.
Tengo un testigo.	I have a witness.

Chapter 01

Page 12: alice_photo/Adobe Stock Photos, muratart/Adobe Stock Photos, Racle Fotodesign/Adobe Stock Photos, Monkey Business/ Adobe Stock Photos, BillionPhotos.com/Adobe Stock Photos, adisa/Adobe Stock Photos, Room 76 Photography/Adobe Stock Photos, monticellllo/Adobe Stock Photos, sumroeng/Adobe Stock Photos, airborne77/Adobe Stock Photos, pressmaster/Adobe Stock Photos, Bits and Splits/Adobe Stock Photos.

Page 13: robin2b/Adobe Stock Photos, Inkara/Adobe Stock Photos, flowertiare/Adobe Stock Photos, Rido/Adobe Stock Photos, RioPatuca Images/Adobe Stock Photos, Artem/Adobe Stock Photos, Robert Wilson/Adobe Stock Photos, Francesco Scatena/Adobe Stock Photos, Rawpixel.com/Adobe Stock Photos, Lotfi MATTOU/Adobe Stock Photos, gstockstudio/Adobe Stock Photos, Svitlana/Adobe Stock Photos.

Page 14: dell/Adobe Stock Photos, nadezhda1906/Adobe Stock Photos, vitaliymateha/Adobe Stock Photos, tonefotografia/Adobe Stock Photos, euthymia/Adobe Stock Photos, Falcon Eyes/Adobe Stock Photos, italita/Adobe Stock Photos, phaisarnwong2517/ Adobe Stock Photos, Maksym Dragunov/Adobe Stock Photos, blacksalmon/Adobe Stock Photos, xy/Adobe Stock Photos, vahe-katrjyan/Adobe Stock Photos.

Page 16: kameraauge/Adobe Stock Photos, mayabuns/Adobe Stock Photos, jarma/Adobe Stock Photos, Scanrail/Adobe Stock Photos, NWM/Adobe Stock Photos, Alice Slee/Adobe Stock Photos, Alessandro Cristiano/Adobe Stock Photos, Nikolai Sorokin/Adobe Stock Photos, Yurii Zushchyk/Adobe Stock Photos, xy/Adobe Stock Photos, jotily/Adobe Stock Photos, stationidea/ Adobe Stock Photos.

Page 17: sultan/Adobe Stock Photos, pakorn/Adobe Stock Photos, adrian_ilie825/Adobe Stock Photos, skyNext/Adobe Stock Photos, kasto/Adobe Stock Photos, EdNurg/Adobe Stock Photos, Sven Grundmann/Adobe Stock Photos, MaxPhotoArt/Adobe Stock Photos, Daniel Ernst/Adobe Stock Photos, auremar/Adobe Stock Photos, pressmaster/Adobe Stock Photos, jdoms/Adobe Stock Photos.

Page 18: #CNF/Adobe Stock Photos, andreusK/Adobe Stock Photos, Kzenon/Adobe Stock Photos, Yakobchuk Olena/Adobe Stock Photos, Uolir/Adobe Stock Photos, littleny/Adobe Stock Photos, gonin/Adobe Stock Photos, jjfarq/Adobe Stock Photos, Vincent Bouchet/Adobe Stock Photos, nerthuz/Adobe Stock Photos, nerthuz/Adobe Stock Photos.

Page 20: Konstantinos Moraiti/Adobe Stock Photos, metelsky25/Adobe Stock Photos, Destina/Adobe Stock Photos, New Africa/Adobe Stock Photos, mipan/Adobe Stock Photos, Sashkin/Adobe Stock Photos, accurate_shot/Adobe Stock Photos, Ayzek/Adobe Stock Photos, kupchynskyi12/Adobe Stock Photos, black_magic/Adobe Stock Photos, GTeam/Adobe Stock Photos, fotofabrika/Adobe Stock Photos.

Page 21: Jürgen Fälchle/Adobe Stock Photos, Laz'e-Pete/Adobe Stock Photos, Pixabay, Nickolay Khoroshkov/Adobe Stock Photos, sp4764/Adobe Stock Photos, Sergey Yarochkin/Adobe Stock Photos, rachid amrous/Adobe Stock Photos, Birgit Reitz-Hofmann/Adobe Stock Photos, rachid amrous/Adobe Stock Photos, biggi62/Adobe Stock Photos, peteri/Adobe Stock Photos, Anton Gvozdikov/Adobe Stock Photos.

Page 22: ERIC/Adobe Stock Photos, bright/Adobe Stock Photos, Alexandra GI/Fotolia, helenedevun/Adobe Stock Photos, Jean-Paul Comparin/Adobe Stock Photos, helenedevun/Adobe Stock Photos, Adrien Roussel/Adobe Stock Photos, graversen36/Adobe Stock Photos, RomainQuéré/Adobe Stock Photos, Chlorophylle/Adobe Stock Photos, fabiomax/Adobe Stock Photos, digitalstock/Adobe Stock Photos.

Page 23: Markus Mainka/Adobe Stock Photos.

Page 24: JackF/Adobe Stock Photos, Rido/Adobe Stock Photos, algre/Adobe Stock Photos, Andrey_Lobachev/Adobe Stock Photos, Konstantinos Moraiti/Adobe Stock Photos, MTG/Adobe Stock Photos, md3d/Adobe Stock Photos, Maksim Toome/Adobe Stock Photos, algre/Adobe Stock Photos, Yuri Bizgaimer/Adobe Stock Photos, Sashkin/Adobe Stock Photos, Norman75/Adobe Stock Photos.

Page 25: ivanko80/Adobe Stock Photos, Flamingo Images/Adobe Stock Photos, Daylight Photo/Adobe Stock Photos.

Page 26: tournee/Adobe Stock Photos, jojoo64/Adobe Stock Photos, Kzenon/Adobe Stock Photos.

Page 27: stockphoto-graf/Adobe Stock Photos, Jiri Hera/Adobe Stock Photos, nito/Adobe Stock Photos, stockphoto-graf/Adobe Stock Photos, rotoGraphics/Adobe Stock Photos, moonrise/Adobe Stock Photos, lastfurianec/Adobe Stock Photos, stock-photo-graf/Adobe Stock Photos, jufo/Adobe Stock Photos, Winai Tepsuttinun/Adobe Stock Photos, philip kinsey/Adobe Stock Photos, Richard Villalon/Adobe Stock Photos.

Page 28: PUNTOSTUDIOFOTO Lda/Adobe Stock Photos, Photobeps/Adobe Stock Photos, ekostsov/Adobe Stock Photos, MIGUEL GARCIA SAAVED/Adobe Stock Photos, nkarol/Adobe Stock Photos, Image'in/Adobe Stock Photos.

Chapter 02

Page 30: Cookie Studio/Adobe Stock Photos, be free/Adobe Stock Photos, Antonioguillem/Adobe Stock Photos, Cookie Studio/Adobe Stock Photos, jackfrog/Adobe Stock Photos, sveta/Adobe Stock Photos, Maridav/Adobe Stock Photos.

Page 32: Viacheslav Iakobchuk/Adobe Stock Photos, Wayhome Studio/Adobe Stock Photos, Wayhome Studio/Adobe Stock Photos, michaelheim/Adobe Stock Photos, Victor Koldunov/Adobe Stock Photos, smallblackcat/Adobe Stock Photos.

Page 33: Maridav/Adobe Stock Photos, detailblick-foto/Adobe Stock Photos, Roman Babakin/Adobe Stock Photos, auremar/Adobe Stock Photos, shurkin_son/Adobe Stock Photos, william87/Adobe Stock Photos.

Page 34: Robert Lehmann/Adobe Stock Photos, StockPhotoAstur/Adobe Stock Photos, rea_molko/Adobe Stock Photos.

Page 35: hin255/Adobe Stock Photos, Oleksandr Moroz/Adobe Stock Photos, Drobot Dean/Adobe Stock Photos, Photo by Djim Loic on Unsplash, devenorr/Adobe Stock Photos, WONG SZE FEI/ Adobe Stock Photos, Prostock-studio/Adobe Stock Photos, WONG SZE FEI/Adobe Stock Photos, Priscilla Du Preez on Unsplash, Jens Ottoson/Adobe Stock Photos, Antonioguillem/Adobe Stock Photos.

Page 36: photobee/Adobe Stock Photos, oneinchpunch/Adobe Stock Photos.

Chapter 03

Page 38: auremar/Adobe Stock Photos, ivanko80/Adobe Stock Photos, Production Perig/Adobe Stock Photos, ilolab/Adobe Stock Photos, ursule/Adobe Stock Photos, rh2010/Adobe Stock Photos, Peter Brewer/Adobe Stock Photos, mk1221/Adobe Stock Photos, asab80/Adobe Stock Photos, Dmytro/Adobe Stock Photos, cantor pannatto/Adobe Stock Photos, eyetronic/Adobe Stock Photos.

Page 39: Brad Pict/Adobe Stock Photos, Johannes Beilharz on Unsplash, Marco2811/Adobe Stock Photos, samott/Adobe Stock Photos, nicknick_ko/Adobe Stock Photos, PHILETDOM/Adobe Stock Photos, kameraauge/Adobe Stock Photos, Eléonore H/ Adobe Stock Photos, alice_photo/Adobe Stock Photos, shiryu01/ Adobe Stock Photos, Kadmy/Adobe Stock Photos, pogonici/Adobe Stock Photos.

Page 40: rlat/Adobe Stock Photos, pressmaster/Adobe Stock Photos.

Page 41: Faruken/Adobe Stock Photos, vladimirfloyd/Adobe Stock Photos, shintartanya/Adobe Stock Photos, methaphum/ Adobe Stock Photos, Antonioguillem/Adobe Stock Photos, PictureP./Adobe Stock Photos, PictureP./Adobe Stock Photos, mantinov/Adobe Stock Photos, Jennifer Coffin-Grey on Unsplash,

New Africa/Adobe Stock Photos, khosrork/Adobe Stock Photos, abidika/Adobe Stock Photos.

Page 42: Alex from the Rock/Adobe Stock Photos, carballo/Adobe Stock Photos, jerome berquez/Adobe Stock Photos.

Page 43: Yasonya/Adobe Stock Photos, s22d/Adobe Stock Photos, jack-sooksan/Adobe Stock Photos, kmiragaya/Adobe Stock Photos, Hervé Rouveure/Adobe Stock Photos, rachid amrous/Adobe Stock Photos, Syda Productions/Adobe Stock Photos, photology1971/Adobe Stock Photos, Gary/Adobe Stock Photos, Lucian Milasan/Adobe Stock Photos, rh2010/Adobe Stock Photos, Annette Schindler/Adobe Stock Photos.

Page 44: Fontanis/Adobe Stock Photos, Heiko Kalweit/Adobe Stock Photos, panosud360/Adobe Stock Photos, valeryegorov/Adobe Stock Photos, Hans-Martin Goede/Adobe Stock Photos, e55evu/Adobe Stock Photos, Karen Grigoryan/Adobe Stock Photos, lago/Adobe Stock Photos, jotily/Adobe Stock Photos, galitskaya/Adobe Stock Photos, Adam Wasilewski/Adobe Stock Photos, Monet/Adobe Stock Photos.

Page 45: zhu difeng/Adobe Stock Photos, zhu difeng/Adobe Stock Photos.

Page 46: martialred/Adobe Stock Photos, martialred/Adobe Stock Photos, martialred/Adobe Stock Photos, martialred/Adobe Stock Photos, Bluejayy/Adobe Stock Photos, martine wagner/Adobe Stock Photos, tradol/Adobe Stock Photos, khuruzero/Adobe Stock Photos, ozaiachin/Adobe Stock Photos.

Page 48: marketlan/Adobe Stock Photos, Oleg/Adobe Stock Photos, vladischern/Adobe Stock Photos, Guillaume Aury/Adobe Stock Photos, Maridav/Adobe Stock Photos, Andreas/Adobe Stock Photos, Cobalt/Adobe Stock Photos, winyu/Adobe Stock Photos, by-studio/Adobe Stock Photos, klagyivik/Adobe Stock Photos, Olesia Bilkei/Adobe Stock Photos, phive2015/Adobe Stock Photos.

Page 49: fred.do.photo/Adobe Stock Photos, saratm/Adobe Stock Photos, sweet tom/Adobe Stock Photos, vansteenwinckel/Adobe Stock Photos.

Page 51: John Smith/Adobe Stock Photos, zlikovec/Adobe Stock Photos, doris oberfrank-list/Adobe Stock Photos, Showcaze/Adobe Stock Photos, Pixxs/Adobe Stock Photos, by-studio/Adobe Stock Photos, sunftaka77/Adobe Stock Photos, s22d/Adobe Stock Photos, Tomo Jesenicnik/Adobe Stock Photos, Cmon/Adobe Stock Photos, Jürgen Fälchle/Adobe Stock Photos, Jeremy/Adobe Stock Photos.

Page 52: panosud360/Adobe Stock Photos, Vera Kuttelvaserova/Adobe Stock Photos, Fineart Panorama/Adobe Stock Photos, motivthueringen8/Adobe Stock Photos.

Page 53: 隆一 本田/Adobe Stock Photos, Marc Andreu/Adobe Stock Photos, resuimages/Adobe Stock Photos, Mike Fouque/Adobe Stock Photos, edan/Adobe Stock Photos, Donnerbold/Adobe Stock Photos, Carl-Jürgen Bautsch/Adobe Stock Photos, annacurnow/Adobe Stock Photos, eloi/Adobe Stock Photos, soundsnaps/Adobe Stock Photos, Netzer Johannes/Adobe Stock Photos, lamax/Adobe Stock Photos.

Page 54: JFL Photography/Adobe Stock Photos, MarcoMonticone/Adobe Stock Photos.

Chapter 04

Page 56: cdrcom/Adobe Stock Photos, leezarius/Adobe Stock Photos, orinocoArt/Adobe Stock Photos, igorkol_ter/Adobe Stock Photos, eshma/Adobe Stock Photos, vvoe/Adobe Stock Photos, vvoe/Adobe Stock Photos, volff/Adobe Stock Photos, Jiri Hera/Adobe Stock Photos.

Page 58: eyetronic/Adobe Stock Photos, PhotoKD/Adobe Stock Photos, coldwaterman/Adobe Stock Photos, Alexander Raths/

Adobe Stock Photos, MarcoBagnoli Elflaco/Adobe Stock Photos, fotoknips/Adobe Stock Photos, Anna/Adobe Stock Photos, Wirestock /Adobe Stock Photos, dream79/Adobe Stock Photos.

Page 59: Joe Gough, Kimberly Reinick/Adobe Stock Photos, illus-trez-vous/Adobe Stock Photos, 5second/Adobe Stock Photos, FomaA/Adobe Stock Photos, Benjamin LEFEBVRE/Adobe Stock Photos, Mara Zemgaliete/Adobe Stock Photos, pavkis/Adobe Stock Photos, Fotofermer/Adobe Stock Photos, jerome Dillard/ Adobe Stock Photos, tashka2000/Adobe Stock Photos, M.studio/ Adobe Stock Photos.

Page 60: Nitr/Adobe Stock Photos, lastsurprise/Adobe Stock Photos, Meryam/Adobe Stock Photos, photocrew/Adobe Stock Photos.

Page 61: M.studio/Adobe Stock Photos, Mara Zemgaliete/ Adobe Stock Photos, MissesJones/Adobe Stock Photos, lefebvre_ jonathan/Adobe Stock Photos, Quade/Adobe Stock Photos, Joe Gough/Adobe Stock Photos, guy/Adobe Stock Photos, Alexander Raths/Adobe Stock Photos, Maurice Metzger/Adobe Stock Photos, ALF photo/Adobe Stock Photos, Dalmatin.o/Adobe Stock Photos, ALF photo/Adobe Stock Photos.

Page 62: eyewave/Adobe Stock Photos, Richard Villalon/Adobe Stock Photos, Laure F/Adobe Stock Photos, goir/Adobe Stock Photos, Sergio Martínez/Adobe Stock Photos, pioneer111/Adobe Stock Photos.

Page 63: whitestorm/Adobe Stock Photos, diamant24/Adobe Stock Photos, Patryk Kosmider/Adobe Stock Photos, jean song/ Adobe Stock Photos, akf/Adobe Stock Photos, Lsantilli/Adobe Stock Photos, ALF photo/Adobe Stock Photos, gitusik/Adobe Stock Photos, Marco Mayer/Adobe Stock Photos, Mara Zemgaliete/ Adobe Stock Photos, lorabarra/Adobe Stock Photos, Bill/Adobe Stock Photos.

Page 64: kab-vision/Adobe Stock Photos, Jérôme Rommé/Adobe Stock Photos, chanelle/Adobe Stock Photos, ChantalS/Adobe Stock Photos, Brad Pict/Adobe Stock Photos, Maceo/Adobe Stock Photos, karelnoppe/Adobe Stock Photos, Volodymyr Shevchuk/Adobe Stock Photos, Sergio Martínez/Adobe Stock Photos, Igor Dudchak/Adobe Stock Photos, Lana Langlois/Adobe Stock Photos, petzshadow/Adobe Stock Photos.

Page 65: L.Bouvier/Adobe Stock Photos, Oleg Zhukov/Adobe Stock Photos.

Page 66: exclusive-design/Adobe Stock Photos, larcobasso/Adobe Stock Photos, gavran333/Adobe Stock Photos, Jiri Hera/Adobe Stock Photos, Iurii Kachkovskyi/Adobe Stock Photos, shibachuu/Adobe Stock Photos, rdnzl/Adobe Stock Photos, lurs/Adobe Stock Photos, ChaoticDesignStudio/Adobe Stock Photos, Pictures news/Adobe Stock Photos, Natika/Adobe Stock Photos, Birgit Reitz-Hofmann/Adobe Stock Photos.

Page 67: Anatoly Repin/Adobe Stock Photos, mariusz_g/Adobe Stock Photos, L.Bouvier/Adobe Stock Photos, shibachuu/Adobe Stock Photos, Lev/Adobe Stock Photos, imagineilona/Adobe Stock Photos, Jiri Hera/Adobe Stock Photos.

Page 68: andriigorulko/Adobe Stock Photos, mbongo/Adobe Stock Photos, osoznaniejizni/Adobe Stock Photos, vitals/Adobe Stock Photos, Moving Moment/Adobe Stock Photos, kitsananan Kuna/Adobe Stock Photos, Silvia Bogdanski/Adobe Stock Photos, Dionisvera/Adobe Stock Photos, Brad Pict/Adobe Stock Photos, Bernard GIRARDIN/Adobe Stock Photos.

Page 69: pixarno/Adobe Stock Photos, Behzadillustration/Adobe Stock Photos, lastsurprise/Adobe Stock Photos, tashka2000/Adobe Stock Photos, FOOD-micro/Adobe Stock Photos, GuillaumeN/Adobe Stock Photos.

Page 70: alinamd/Adobe Stock Photos, Voravuth/Adobe Stock Photos, Ian 2010/Adobe Stock Photos, atoss/Adobe Stock Photos, atoss/Adobe Stock Photos, ChaoticDesignStudio/Adobe Stock Photos, grey/Adobe Stock Photos, volff/Adobe Stock Photos, valery121283/Adobe Stock Photos, volff/Adobe Stock Photos, kovaleva_ka/Adobe Stock Photos, atoss/Adobe Stock Photos.

Page 71: bestphotostudio/Adobe Stock Photos, yvdavid/Adobe Stock Photos, Serhiy Shullye/Adobe Stock Photos, anders-photo/Adobe Stock Photos, Alexstar/Adobe Stock Photos, alexlukin/Adobe Stock Photos, Adobe Systems Incorporated, Iurii Kachkovskyi/Adobe Stock Photos, Alexandr Vlassyuk/Adobe Stock Photos, Natika/Adobe Stock Photos, Anna Sedneva/Adobe Stock Photos, kovaleva_ka/Adobe Stock Photos.

Page 72: akamaraqu/Adobe Stock Photos, Mariusz Blach/Adobe Stock Photos, illustrez-vous/Adobe Stock Photos, L.Bouvier/Adobe Stock Photos, Pixel-Shot/Adobe Stock Photos, Pixel-Shot/Adobe Stock Photos, Tim UR/Adobe Stock Photos, guitou60/Adobe Stock Photos, Thierry Hoarau/Adobe Stock Photos, Yeti Studio/Adobe Stock Photos, Zipo/Adobe Stock Photos.

Page 73: janvier/Adobe Stock Photos, Gresei/Adobe Stock Photos, freila/Adobe Stock Photos, stefanoventuri/Adobe Stock Photos, SunnyS/Adobe Stock Photos, xamtiw/Adobe Stock Photos, stockphoto-graf/Adobe Stock Photos, luissybuster/Adobe Stock Photos, Hyrma/Adobe Stock Photos, duncanandison/Adobe Stock Photos, Barbara Pheby/Adobe Stock Photos, Xavier/Adobe Stock Photos.

Page 74: oleh11/Adobe Stock Photos, Valentina R./Adobe Stock Photos, Superheang168/Adobe Stock Photos, margo555/Adobe Stock Photos, Scisetti Alfio/Adobe Stock Photos, Jörg Rautenberg/Adobe Stock Photos, nd700/Adobe Stock Photos, Viktor/Adobe Stock Photos, sucharat/Adobe Stock Photos, Angel Simon/Adobe Stock Photos, robert6666/Adobe Stock Photos, Natika/Adobe Stock Photos.

Page 75: Scisetti Alfio/Adobe Stock Photos, andriigorulko/Adobe Stock Photos, Nataly-Nete/Adobe Stock Photos, Dionisvera/ Adobe Stock Photos, womue/Adobe Stock Photos, constantinos/ Adobe Stock Photos.

Page 76: Konstiantyn/Adobe Stock Photos, puhhha/Adobe Stock Photos, DAVID/Adobe Stock Photos, bramgino/Adobe Stock Photos, Monique Pouzet/Adobe Stock Photos, Ilshat/ Adobe Stock Photos, arinahabich/Adobe Stock Photos, Irina Schmidt/Adobe Stock Photos.

Page 77: EdNurg/Adobe Stock Photos, kubais/Adobe Stock Photos, twixx/Adobe Stock Photos, murasal/Adobe Stock Photos, Syda Productions/Adobe Stock Photos, estradaanton/Adobe Stock Photos, johnmerlin/Adobe Stock Photos, luckypic/Adobe Stock Photos.

Page 79: Gresei/Adobe Stock Photos, annapustynnikova/Adobe Stock Photos, cdrcom/Adobe Stock Photos, Sergio Martínez/ Adobe Stock Photos, Richard Villalon/Adobe Stock Photos, Africa Studio/Adobe Stock Photos, vitals/Adobe Stock Photos, PhotoSG/ Adobe Stock Photos, andersphoto/Adobe Stock Photos, Sergio Martínez/Adobe Stock Photos.

Page 80: Sergio Martínez/Adobe Stock Photos, Mara Zemgaliete/ Adobe Stock Photos, ALF photo/Adobe Stock Photos, Ryzhkov/ Adobe Stock Photos, Sergio Martínez/Adobe Stock Photos, Xavier/Adobe Stock Photos, Fernando Cortés/Adobe Stock Photos, Mara Zemgaliete/Adobe Stock Photos, uckyo/Adobe Stock Photos, guy/Adobe Stock Photos, nito/Adobe Stock Photos, Sergio Martínez/Adobe Stock Photos.

Page 81: Nickske/Adobe Stock Photos, Sergio Martínez/Adobe Stock Photos.

Page 82: dream79/Adobe Stock Photos, alinamd/Adobe Stock Photos, ampFotoStudio.com/Adobe Stock Photos, Gaetan Soupa/Adobe Stock Photos, Lsantilli/Adobe Stock Photos, Sergio

Martínez/Adobe Stock Photos, M.studio/Adobe Stock Photos, rockvillephoto/Adobe Stock Photos, Adobe Systems Incorporated, helenedevun/Adobe Stock Photos, unpict/Adobe Stock Photos, Brad Pict/Adobe Stock Photos.

Page 83: photocrew/Adobe Stock Photos, Richard Villalon/Adobe Stock Photos, viperagp/Adobe Stock Photos, emuck/Adobe Stock Photos, FomaA/Adobe Stock Photos, nito/Adobe Stock Photos, Africa Studio/Adobe Stock Photos, mariontxa/Adobe Stock Photos.

Page 84: barbulat/Adobe Stock Photos, san_ta/Adobe Stock Photos, zothen/Adobe Stock Photos.

Page 85: Maximo Sanz/Adobe Stock Photos, sum41/Adobe Stock Photos, picsfive/Adobe Stock Photos, Vladislav Nosik/Adobe Stock Photos, exclusive-design/Adobe Stock Photos, Dmitry Naumov/Adobe Stock Photos, Jenifoto/Adobe Stock Photos, fahrwasser/Adobe Stock Photos, Marco2811/Adobe Stock Photos, dimakp/Adobe Stock Photos, NoahGolan/Adobe Stock Photos, sunwaylight13/Adobe Stock Photos.

Page 86: M.studio/Adobe Stock Photos, rudisetiawan/Adobe Stock Photos, frogstyle/Adobe Stock Photos.

Page 87: Luminis/Adobe Stock Photos, Elenathewise/Adobe Stock Photos, alefat/Adobe Stock Photos, Mariyana M/Adobe Stock Photos, belinot/Adobe Stock Photos, Cristal Oscuro/Adobe Stock Photos, by-studio/Adobe Stock Photos, Robert Latawiec/Adobe Stock Photos, boomeart/Adobe Stock Photos, Ezio Gutzemberg/Adobe Stock Photos, Nigel Monckton/Adobe Stock Photos, Dmitry Ersler/Adobe Stock Photos.

Page 88: He2/Adobe Stock Photos, Nutthawut Paenthong/Adobe Stock Photos, Alexandr Steblovskiy/Adobe Stock Photos, 5ph/Adobe Stock Photos, pepebaeza/Adobe Stock Photos, Brent Hofacker/Adobe Stock Photos.

Page 89: EastWest Imaging/Adobe Stock Photos, Eisenhans/Adobe Stock Photos, Andrey Popov/Adobe Stock Photos, Julie LEGRAND/Adobe Stock Photos, Ideenkoch/Adobe Stock Photos, qech/Adobe Stock Photos, Jürgen Priewe/Adobe Stock Photos.

Chapter 05

Page 92: Diana Rui/Adobe Stock Photos, dglimages/Adobe Stock Photos, dit26978/Adobe Stock Photos, kitthanes/Adobe Stock Photos, triocean/Adobe Stock Photos, bebeball/Adobe Stock Photos, Andrey Popov/Adobe Stock Photos, New Africa/Adobe Stock Photos, New Africa/Adobe Stock Photos, Pixel-Shot/Adobe Stock Photos.

Page 93: Alex Tihonov/Adobe Stock Photos, Alex Tihonov/Adobe Stock Photos, modernmovie/Adobe Stock Photos, mmphoto/Adobe Stock Photos, joserpizarro/Adobe Stock Photos, Rawpixel.com/Adobe Stock Photos, aberenyi/Adobe Stock Photos, Konstantin L/Adobe Stock Photos, Pixel-Shot/Adobe Stock Photos, andreusK/Adobe Stock Photos.

Page 95: corvalola/Adobe Stock Photos, chinnarach/Adobe Stock Photos, Looker_Studio/Adobe Stock Photos, Piman Khrutmuang/Adobe Stock Photos, Pixel-Shot/Adobe Stock Photos, phonlamai-photo/Adobe Stock Photos, piyaphunjun/Adobe Stock Photos, Goffkein/Adobe Stock Photos, Jason/Adobe Stock Photos, comzeal/Adobe Stock Photos, Simon Coste/Adobe Stock Photos.

Page 96: Alex Tihonov/Adobe Stock Photos, Kalim/Adobe Stock Photos, ValentinValkov/Adobe Stock Photos, Tryfonov/Adobe Stock Photos, sumroeng/Adobe Stock Photos, Africa Studio/Adobe Stock Photos, ChenPG/Adobe Stock Photos, mario beau-regard/Adobe Stock Photos, _jure/Adobe Stock Photos, Kzenon/Adobe Stock Photos, Gstudio/Adobe Stock Photos.

Page 98: andreusK/Adobe Stock Photos, robepco/Adobe Stock Photos, Roman Babakin/Adobe Stock Photos, abramsdesign/Adobe Stock Photos, Sharon/Adobe Stock Photos, Nastasia Froloff/Adobe Stock Photos, Deyan Georgiev/Adobe Stock

Photos, Mark Herreid/Fotolia, rootstocks/Adobe Stock Photos, Rawf8/Adobe Stock Photos, Photo Feats/Adobe Stock Photos, anatoliy_gleb/Adobe Stock Photos.

Page 99: Hyrma/Adobe Stock Photos, BublikHaus/Adobe Stock Photos, Vaceslav Romanov/Adobe Stock Photos, andriano_cz/Adobe Stock Photos, solidmaks/Adobe Stock Photos, BillionPhotos.com/Adobe Stock Photos, arthito/Adobe Stock Photos, PhotoKD/Adobe Stock Photos.

Page 101: ArchiVIZ/Adobe Stock Photos, Pascal Huot/Adobe Stock Photos, Iriana Shiyan/Adobe Stock Photos, Prostock-studio/Adobe Stock Photos, tktktk/Adobe Stock Photos, Pixel-Shot/Adobe Stock Photos, StockOption/Adobe Stock Photos, nick_fedirko/Adobe Stock Photos, pics721/Adobe Stock Photos, maryviolet/Adobe Stock Photos, Jonathan Stutz/Adobe Stock Photos, Arunee/Adobe Stock Photos.

Page 102: oktay/Adobe Stock, Victor/Adobe Stock Photos, Carsten Reisinger/Adobe Stock Photos, Oligo/Adobe Stock Photos, martialred/Adobe Stock Photos, mariesacha/Adobe Stock Photos, Leigh Prather/Adobe Stock Photos, alexnikit/Adobe Stock, abrams-design/Adobe Stock Photos, leszekglasner/Adobe Stock Photos, New Africa/Adobe Stock Photos, Goffkein/Adobe Stock Photos.

Page 103: Onidji/Adobe Stock Photos, brizmaker/Adobe Stock Photos, nikkytok/Adobe Stock Photos, auremar/Adobe Stock Photos, Eléonore H/Adobe Stock Photos, FollowTheFlow/Adobe Stock Photos, gamespirit/Adobe Stock Photos, mariesacha/Adobe Stock Photos, MoiraM/Adobe Stock Photos.

Page 105: Javani LLC/Adobe Stock Photos, navintar/Adobe Stock Photos, pjjaruwan/Adobe Stock Photos, Mariusz Blach/Adobe Stock Photos, ILYA AKINSHIN/Adobe Stock Photos, ddukang/Adobe Stock Photos, Rinku/Adobe Stock Photos, Panama/Adobe Stock Photos, khuruzero/Adobe Stock Photos, Photographee.eu/Adobe Stock Photos, ILYA AKINSHIN/Adobe Stock Photos, Anton84/Adobe Stock Photos.

Page 106: maykal/Adobe Stock Photos, faraktinov/Adobe Stock Photos, chatchawan/Adobe Stock Photos, Madeleine Steinbach/ Adobe Stock Photos, Pixel-Shot/Adobe Stock Photos, Yakobchuk Olena/Adobe Stock Photos, AlenKadr/Adobe Stock Photos, Kuzmick/Adobe Stock Photos, timothyh/Adobe Stock Photos, martialred/Adobe Stock Photos, Sergey Skleznev/Adobe Stock Photos, Larry Allen Peplin/Adobe Stock Photos.

Page 107: Nitr/Adobe Stock Photos.

Chapter 06

Page 110: alexlmx/Adobe Stock Photos, Vladimir Gerasimov/ Adobe Stock Photos, visart/Adobe Stock Photos, Kenishirotie/ Adobe Stock Photos, darren415/Adobe Stock Photos, Julydfg/ Adobe Stock Photos, chrisdorney/Adobe Stock Photos.

Page 112: New Africa/Adobe Stock Photos, StudioStoltz/Adobe Stock Photos, VAKSMANV/Adobe Stock Photos, Eulalia Cayuela Martinez/Adobe Stock Photos, Richard Villalon/Adobe Stock Photos, Chandler/Adobe Stock Photos, Jacob Lund/Adobe Stock Photos, Frog974/Adobe stock Photos, studiocasper/ Adobe Stock Photos, industrieblick/Adobe Stock Photos, motortion/Adobe Stock Photos.

Page 113: Antonio/Adobe Stock Photos, Syda Production/Adobe Stock Photos.

Page 114: daniilvolkov/Adobe Stock Photos, Anthony SEJOURNE/ Adobe Stock Photos, chinaface/ Adobe Stock Photos, Prostock-studio/Adobe Stock Photos, Pgiam/ Adobe Stock Photos, Photo by Paweł Bukowski/Unsplash, bigy9950/Adobe Stock Photos, Herbivore/Adobe Stock Photos, monticellllo/Adobe Stock Photos, Dario Lo Presti/Adobe Stock Photos, JackF/Adobe Stock Photos; herraez/Adobe Stock Photos.

Page 115: Photoagriculture/Adobe Stock Photos, JackF/Adobe Stock Photos, Kondor83/ Adobe Stock Photos, sergantstar/Adobe

Stock Photos, KCULP/Adobe Stock Photos, Adrienne/Adobe Stock Photos, funky-data/ Adobe Stock Photos, deepblue4you/ Adobe Stock Photos, Prostock-studio/Adobe Stock Photos, Anouchka/ Adobe Stock Photos, iStock.com/vasiliki, IGphotography/ Adobe Stock Photos.

Page 116: New Africa/Adobe Stock Photos.

Page 117: Image'in/Adobe Stock Photos, alexsl/ Adobe Stock Photos, mipan/Adobe Stock Photos, lisinski/ Adobe Stock Photos, Image'in/Adobe Stock Photos, phonlamaiphoto/Adobe Stock Photos, WavebreakmediaMicro/Adobe Stock Photos, industrie-blick/Adobe Stock Photos, seanami/ Adobe Stock Photos, Guven Polat/ Adobe Stock Photos, skampixelle/Adobe Stock Photos, M.studio/Adobe Stock Photos.

Page 118: Kondor83/Adobe Stock Photos, Christophe Fouquin/ Adobe Stock Photos, sonyakamoz/Adobe Stock Photos, Pixabay, JackF/Adobe Stock Photos.

Page 119: Timmary/Adobe Stock Photos, jon_chica/Adobe Stock Photos, kobeza/Adobe Stock Photos, Unclesam/Adobe Stock Photos, Marc Roche/Adobe Stock Photos, Silvio/Adobe Stock Photos, RomainQuéré/Adobe Stock Photos, nito/Adobe Stock Photos, emuck/Adobe Stock Photos, Gaetan Soupa/Adobe Stock Photos, Maciej Czekajewski/Adobe Stock Photos, helenedevun/Adobe Stock Photos.

Page 120: Kenjo/Adobe Stock Photos.

Page 121: nito/Adobe Stock Photos, ksena32/Istockphoto, koce-toilief/ Adobe Stock Photos, aimy27feb/Adobe Stock Photos, arts/ Adobe Stock Photos, Khvost/Adobe Stock Photos, Ruslan Kudrin/ Adobe Stock Photos, ucmao from Pixabay, Alex Green/Adobe Stock Photos, Tarzhanova/Adobe Stock Photos, Tarzhanova/ Adobe Stock Photos, mstudio/Adobe Stock Photos.

Page 122: Pixabay, Tarzhanova/Adobe Stock Photos, demidoff/Adobe Stock Photos, Khvost/Adobe Stock Photos, Dmytro Sandratskyi/Adobe Stock Photos, markasia/Adobe Stock Photos, Drobot Dean/Adobe Stock Photos, srki66/Adobe Stock Photos, serbogachuk/Adobe Stock Photos, Muenchbach/Adobe Stock Photos, Valentin/Adobe Stock Photos, Alexandra_K/Adobe Stock Photos.

Page 123: Adobe Stock Photos, pixarno/Adobe Stock Photos, sumire8/Adobe Stock Photos, Argus/Adobe Stock Photos, wabeno/Adobe Stock Photos, Dmitriy Syechin/Adobe Stock Photos, strichpunkt/Pixabay, pkleindienst/Adobe Stock Photos, CNF Vector/Pixabay, DavidZydd/Pixabay, nata777_7/Adobe Stock Photos, mubus/Adobe Stock Photos.

Page 124: srckomkrit/Adobe Stock Photos, ovindji/Adobe Stock Photos, OneClic/Adobe Stock Photos, Anna/Adobe Stock Photos, malven/Adobe Stock Photos, TATTU/Adobe Stock Photos, OneClic/Adobe Stock Photos, Simone Schuldis/Adobe Stock Photos, OneClic/Adobe Stock Photos, slay19/Adobe Stock Photos.

Page 126: Tydav Photos/Adobe Stock Photos, Popova Olga/Adobe Stock Photos, nata777_7/Adobe Stock Photos, luckybusiness/Adobe Stock Photos, Dmitriy Golbay/Adobe Stock Photos, martina87/Adobe Stock Photos, New Africa/Adobe Stock Photos, Sergii Gnatiuk/ Adobe Stock Photos, ksena32/Adobe Stock Photos, pixelrobot/Adobe Stock Photos, Africa Studio/Adobe Stock Photos, uwimages/Adobe Stock Photos.

Page 127: Kybele/Adobe Stock Photos, Valerii Zan/Adobe Stock Photos, roman_baiadin/Adobe Stock Photos.

Page 128: gennadiy75/Adobe Stock Photos, MikeBiTa/Adobe Stock Photos, Tanya Rozhnovskaya/Adobe Stock Photos, abramsdesign/Adobe Stock Photos, StockSnap/Pixabay, photoblink/Adobe Stock Photos, StockSnap/Pixabay, cipariss/Adobe Stock Photos, sombats/Adobe Stock Photos, sombats/Adobe Stock Photos, Manish Patanwar/Adobe Stock Photos, Etaphop photo/Adobe Stock Photos.

Page 129: Andrzej Tokarski/Adobe Stock Photos, Pexels, Pixabay, katrin_timoff/Adobe Stock Photos, Joachim Roth/Adobe Stock Photos, foxdammit/Adobe Stock Photos, foxdammit/Adobe Stock Photos.

Page 130: nyurgun/Adobe Stock Photos, philippe Devanne// Adobe Stock Photos, M W/Pixabay, Skitterphoto/Pexels, Emma Larocque/Pixabay, EdNurg/Adobe Stock Photos, Simon/Pixabay, Elsemargriet/Pixabay, Holger Schué/Pixabay, YuricBel/Adobe Stock Photos, Kybele/Adobe Stock Photos, Catherine CLAVERY/ Adobe Stock Photos.

Page 131: Reinhold Silbermann/Pixabay, Hans Braxmeier/ Pixabay, zhukovvvlad/Adobe Stock Photos, StockSnap/Pixabay, edan/Adobe Stock Photos, Donnerbold/Adobe Stock Photos, par Rudy and Peter Skitterians/Pixabay, NDABCREATIVITY/Adobe Stock Photos, Barry Jones/Pixabay, Z2A1/Adobe Stock Photos, famveldman/Adobe Stock Photos, Rémy MASSEGLIA/Adobe Stock Photos.

Page 132: Jérôme Castel/Adobe Stock Photos, helivideo/Adobe Stock Photos, Pexels/Pixabay, Kevin Phillips/Pixabay, anekoho/ Adobe Stock Photos, Mustafa Kücük - v. Gruenewaldt/Pixabay, jarmoluk/Pixabay, pololia/Adobe Stock Photos, marino/Adobe Stock Photos, RealCG/Adobe Stock Photos, mirkomedia/Adobe Stock Photos, WavebreakmediaMicro/Adobe Stock Photos.

Page 133: Pixabay, Stefan Schurr/Adobe Stock Photos, Cynthiamcastro/Pixabay, Gerd Funcke/Pixabay, Michael Schwarzenberger/Pixabay, Y. L. Photographies/Adobe Stock Photos, Francis Lempérière/Adobe Stock Photos.

Page 134: MB/Adobe Stock Photos, AndiP/Pixabay, Dusan Kostic/Adobe Stock Photos, razihusin/Adobe Stock Photos, Keith Johnston/Pixabay, vectorfusionart/Adobe Stock Photos, Kzenon/Adobe Stock Photos, italo/Adobe Stock Photos, Celestine Ekpenyong/Pixabay, fovivafoto/Adobe Stock Photos, olly/Adobe Stock Photos.

Page 135: pixtour/Adobe Stock Photos, xpixel/ Adobe Stock Photos, MARIMA/Adobe Stock Photos, makasana photo/Adobe Stock Photos, Fly_and_Dive/Adobe Stock Photos, adaptice/Adobe Stock Photos, Tomfry/Adobe Stock Photos, Charles de Lisle/ Adobe Stock Photos, Sylvain TANGUY/Adobe Stock Photos, Didier San Martin/Adobe Stock Photos, Camila Cordeiro/Unsplash, uwimages/Adobe Stock Photos.

Page 136: Wonderful pictures/Adobe Stock Photos, tudiopromo-mobile/Pixabay, Dimitris Vetsikas/Pixabay, SplitShire/Pixabay, Gerhard G./Pixabay, pixelrobot/Adobe Stock Photos, István Kis/ Pixabay, itsallgood/Adobe Stock Photos, Christine JAMIN/Pixabay, Franck Thomasse/Adobe Stock Photos, haveseen/Adobe Stock Photos, PublicDomainPictures/Pixabay.

Page 137: David D/Pixabay, Rostislav Ageev/Adobe Stock Photos, jacqueline macou/Pixabay, itsallgood/Adobe Stock Photos, ALF photo/Adobe Stock Photos, Yay Images/Adobe Stock Photos, Manfred Antranias Zimmer/Pixabay, mma23/Adobe Stock Photos.

Page 139: shocky/Adobe Stock Photos, summa/Pixabay, Tania Van den Berghen/Pixabay, Africa Studio/Adobe Stock Photos, Jan Haerer/Pixabay, Steve Buissinne/Pixabay, MichaelM/Pixabay, AlcelVision/Adobe Stock Photos.

Page 141: Artem Furman/Adobe Stock Photos, auremar/Adobe Stock Photos, IvicaNS/Adobe Stock Photos, Denis Rozhnovsky/ Adobe Stock Photos, artem_goncharov/Adobe Stock Photos, Gowtham/Adobe Stock Photos.

Page 142: metamorworks/Adobe Stock Photos, David Franklin/ Adobe Stock Photos, andrys lukowski/Adobe Stock Photos, ZoneCreative/Adobe Stock Photos, Yay Images/Adobe Stock Photos, Anton Gvozdikov/Adobe Stock Photos, altomedia/Adobe Stock Photos, LAURENT VICENZOTTI/Adobe Stock Photos, VIAR PRO studio/Adobe Stock Photos, The History Collection/Adobe Stock Photos, Orlando Florin Rosu/Adobe Stock Photos.

Page 143: Gary/Adobe Stock Photos, Pixabay, Chlorophylle/ Adobe Stock Photos, Juan Enrique Soto/Adobe Stock Photos, Andy-pix/Adobe Stock Photos, Jan Rose/Adobe Stock Photos, yunje5054/12 Bilder/Pixabay, kozlik_mozlik/Adobe Stock Photos, Artem Furman/Adobe Stock Photos, Pixabay, Africa Studio/Adobe Stock Photos, shocky/Adobe Stock Photos.

Page 144: phonlamaiphoto/Adobe Stock Photos, sapsan777/ Adobe Stock Photos, small tom/Adobe Stock Photos, Nikolai Sorokin/Adobe Stock Photos, crushmaster/Adobe Stock Photos, James Steidl/Adobe Stock Photos, AGCuesta/Adobe Stock Photos, aleksandarfilip/Adobe Stock Photos, AGCuesta/Adobe Stock Photos, small tom/Adobe Stock Photos, Pixabay, RomainQuéré/ Adobe Stock Photos.

Page 145: Adobe Stock Photos, niekverlaan/349 images/Pixabay.

Page 146: Monkey Business/Adobe Stock Photos, Africa Studio/ Adobe Stock Photos, 4th Life Photography/Adobe Stock Photos, Redzen/Adobe Stock Photos, Pavel Losevsky/Adobe Stock Photos, Vladimir Wrangel/Adobe Stock Photos, Photographee.eu/Adobe Stock Photos, Jeffery/Adobe Stock Photos, Erica Guilane-Nachez/ Adobe Stock Photos, Ispasl/ Adobe Stock Photos, Serjio/Adobe Stock Photos.

Page 148: Alisson/Adobe Stock Photos, Viacheslav Iakobchuk/ Adobe Stock Photos, Pixabay, Jérôme Rommé/Adobe Stock Photos, Carlos Valera/Adobe Stock Photos, Pavel Losevsky/Adobe Stock Photos, Jonathan Stutz/Adobe Stock Photos, regis/Adobe Stock Photos, KABUGUI/Adobe Stock Photos, bARTiko/Adobe Stock Photos, wikorba/Adobe Stock Photos, Toanet/Adobe Stock Photos.

Chapter 07

Page 152: Rido/Adobe Stock Photos, simmittorok/Adobe Stock Photos, vladimirfloyd/Adobe Stock Photos, anjocreatif/Adobe Stock Photos, razoomanetu/Adobe Stock Photos, LoloStock/

Adobe Stock Photos, littlestocker/Adobe Stock Photos, Krakenimages.com/Adobe Stock Photos, filistimlyanin1/Adobe Stock Photos, kaymotec/Adobe Stock Photos, Zemler/Adobe Stock Photos, mraoraor/Adobe Stock Photos.

Page 153: exzozis/Adobe Stock Photos, luengo_ua/Adobe Stock Photos, SciePro/Adobe Stock Photos, mraoraor/Adobe Stock Photos, volff/Adobe Stock Photos, mraoraor/Adobe Stock Photos, WavebreakmediaMicro/Adobe Stock Photos, Glebstock/Adobe Stock Photos, vladimirfloyd/Adobe Stock Photos, HANK GREBE/ Adobe Stock Photos, Anatomy Insider/Adobe Stock Photos, SciePro/Adobe Stock Photos.

Page 154: SciePro/Adobe Stock Photos, sema_srinouljan/Adobe Stock Photos, Proxima Studio/Adobe Stock Photos, dream@do/Adobe Stock Photos, alexlmx/Adobe Stock Photos, Maksym Yemelyanov/Adobe Stock Photos, SciePro/Adobe Stock Photos, eranicle/Adobe Stock Photos, Rasi/Adobe Stock Photos, SciePro/ Adobe Stock Photos.

Page 155: maru54/Adobe Stock Photos, kei907/Adobe Stock Photos, deagreez/Adobe Stock Photos, Cookie Studio/Adobe Stock Photos, narongchaihlaw/Adobe Stock Photos, Liudmila Dutko/Adobe Stock Photos, elavuk81/Adobe Stock Photos, schankz/Adobe Stock Photos, blackday/Adobe Stock Photos, Syda Productions/Adobe Stock Photos, asierromero/Adobe Stock Photos, Микола Ковальчинськи/Adobe Stock Photos.

Page 156: schankz/Adobe Stock Photos, PixieMe/Adobe Stock Photos, icsnaps/Adobe Stock Photos, booleen/Adobe Stock Photos, gstockstudio/Adobe Stock Photos, belokrylowa/Adobe Stock Photos, Anatoliy Karlyuk/Adobe Stock Photos.

Page 157: photowahn/Adobe Stock Photos, bnenin/Adobe Stock Photos, Simone van den Berg/Adobe Stock Photos, auremar/ Adobe Stock Photos, Pixel-Shot/Adobe Stock Photos, dalaprod/ Adobe Stock Photos, RomainQuéré/Adobe Stock Photos, drubig-photo/Adobe Stock Photos, rogerphoto/Adobe Stock Photos.

Page 159: emiliau/Adobe Stock Photos, Goffkein/Adobe Stock Photos, John Neff/Adobe Stock Photos, Open Art/Adobe Stock Photos, sementsova321/Adobe Stock Photos, metamorworks/Adobe Stock Photos, Andrey Popov/Adobe Stock Photos, gallofilm/Adobe Stock Photos, master1305/Adobe Stock Photos, Racle Fotodesign/Adobe Stock Photos, tugolukof/Adobe Stock Photos, zinkevych/Adobe Stock Photos.

Page 160: RFBSIP/Adobe Stock Photos, sebra/Adobe Stock Photos, Andrey Popov/Adobe Stock Photos, Richard Villalon/Adobe Stock Photos, piXuLariUm/Adobe Stock Photos, Ariane Citron/Adobe Stock Photos, alexmak/Adobe Stock Photos, bellakadife/Adobe Stock Photos, Ольга Тернавская/Adobe Stock Photos, STUDIO GRAND WEB/Adobe Stock Photos, michaelheim/Adobe Stock Photos, andriano_cz/Adobe Stock Photos.

Page 162: Tyler Olson/Adobe Stock Photos, Kadmy/Adobe Stock Photos, Andy Dean/Adobe Stock Photos, photophonie/Adobe Stock Photos, BestForYou/Adobe Stock Photos, Jasmina/Adobe Stock Photos, James Thew/Adobe Stock Photos, Jiri Hera/Adobe Stock Photos, Ketmut/Adobe Stock Photos, azure/Adobe Stock Photos, DW labs Incorporated/Adobe Stock Photos, nevodka.com/Adobe Stock Photos.

Page 163: Voyagerix/Adobe Stock Photos, Юлия Пипкина/Adobe Stock Photos, sommai/Adobe Stock Photos, Joachim/Adobe Stock Photos, gna60/Adobe Stock Photos, Andrzej Wilusz/Adobe Stock Photos, Coprid/Adobe Stock Photos, Richard Villalon/Adobe Stock Photos, Coprid/Adobe Stock Photos.

Page 165: upixa/Adobe Stock Photos, xiaosan/Adobe Stock Photos, Robert Hainer/Adobe Stock Photos, Joaquin Corbalan/Adobe Stock Photos, bunyos/fotolia, Richard Villalon/Adobe Stock Photos, sveta/Adobe Stock Photos, Gennadiy Poznyakov/Fotolia LLC, shutterdemon/Adobe Stock Photos, rh2010/Adobe Stock Photos, Kurhan/Adobe Stock Photos, romaset/Adobe Stock Photos.

Page 166: Jacob Lund/Adobe Stock Photos, Jacob Lund/Adobe Stock Photos, Liliia/Adobe Stock Photos.

Page 167: Lidia_Lo/Adobe Stock Photos, David San Segundo/Adobe Stock Photos, Dimco/Adobe Stock Photos, Vivvi Smak/Adobe Stock Photos, carballo/Adobe Stock Photos, petzshadow/Adobe Stock Photos, Johnstocker/Adobe Stock Photos, Pixel-Shot/Adobe Stock Photos, Inkara/Adobe Stock Photos, onephoto/Adobe Stock Photos, fmalot/Adobe Stock Photos, martinprague/Adobe Stock Photos.